The Silent Journey

GW00481880

Michael J. Bellito

Strategic Book Publishing and Rights Co.

Strategic Book Publishing and Rights Co., LLC
USA | Singapore
www.sbpra.net

For information about special discounts for bulk purchases, please contact Strategic Book Publishing and Rights Co. Special Sales, at bookorder@sbpra.net.

ISBN: 978-1-68181-727-9

Book Design: Suzanne Kelly

To all the therapists who helped me:
especially Kyle, Sue, and Kristina.

To all the people that helped me the most: Matt,
Becki, Luke, Ryan, Stephen, Joy, Charlotte, Andrew,
Milo, Mom, and Mr. Moon.

And to the woman I would not be here without:
Joani, my wife.

To my all-time editor, who steadfastly reads
for errors: Erin Brooks

PREFACE

Hi, folks. Well, this is it. A non-fiction narrative typed (with my left hand) all about my stroke and the curative powers I gained from it. I wouldn't want you to think I would wish this on any person, but I have to say I have grown from it, slowly but surely. Read every chapter and see, if you can, the heartfelt grief I experienced with the stroke. And then, the sense of relief I felt with every step I took in this incredible journey.

I decided to name it *The Silent Journey.* This was because I never knew that one thing you lost, with some strokes, was your ability to speak. I lost not only my voice, but my career as a teacher. This I miss, and would be doing it still if I could. Well, after forty years of doing what I truly love, it was probably time for a break.

I want to take a minute to thank the therapists, all of them. If it weren't for their hard and tireless work, I wouldn't be here. They are masters at what they do.

Last of all, I want to thank my wife, Joani. She knows how hard it's been. And she never, ever gives up.

It's not hard to write about your past memories. I've decided to write about my present goings-on. Well, read on. I hope you enjoy it.

CHAPTER 1

It was a wild week. On Wednesday night, Allyssa had gone to bed, too tired to even stay up past eight to watch the animal show. We were chatting with Katie, mostly about her upcoming year at Taylor University, when the doorbell rang. I glanced at Joani, my wife of thirty-six years, to see if she was expecting someone; she wasn't. I made my way to the front door. I thought as I walked that it had been a tiresome week, with the three girls staying overnight for the Spring Hill Summer Camp, to be held at our church. I opened the door; there stood a man and his dog that I had never seen before, although we'd lived in the neighborhood for almost twenty-nine years. There was no wind to speak of, which made the statement the man made that much more amazing. "I was out walking my dog," the stranger said. "I heard a loud crash, and turned to see a big tree branch fall on your car."

It took only a minute to see the proof; Allyssa's car was smashed beyond recognition. It took a brave Katie to wake up Allyssa and haul her out to the car. Joani called up "Big Bob," a neighbor who at first didn't believe her; then he accepted her blunt truth.

Once a catastrophe occurred, all our friendly neighbors came out to look. The neighbors got to work fast, a chainsaw doing the bulk of the work, as Allyssa watched in horror, comforted by Alexandra, the third girl in the trio. Once the bulk of the wood had been set aside, Allyssa's car could be looked at. It didn't look as bad as had first been imagined. Only the windshield was broken beyond hope, and a good repairman could fix it in a jiffy. "Big Bob" called his insurance man, and we all climbed into bed, where we slept like infants, Allyssa being the sole exception.

The next morning shone bright and clear. Sarah, the leader, picked the girls up before seven, so they could be to church on time. The next day Alexandra had to be taken to the hospital for observation. She was suffering from a type of brain cancer, and the tiredness from this week and all the other weeks combined had made her give in. We were beginning to wonder whether we should have had these three girls stay at our house.

The repairman came in the afternoon to fix the windshield. It would take him a good amount of time. Meanwhile, Luke and Ryan, our identical twin grandsons, came to play. Matt, their dad, drove them over. We played the usual games: hide-and-seek, tag, and search for the wild animals. At three years old, they were every bit as troublesome as you would expect them to be.

They were as curious as ever about the windshield. They stared at the man as he worked away, struggling to identify the cause of the broken windowpane. I took them over to see the cord of wood, laid out on the ground, and that seemed to satisfy them.

I had to chase them once when they caught sight of the rabbit that had been eating his mornings away at my strawberry patch; needless to say, the wired rabbit ran faster than the boys. Having shagged them back, I coaxed them into the house for some fruit snacks. Ryan, always the thinker, came up with a novel idea, pounding his hand in his fist as he spoke. "Luke and I will catch that rabbit for you. And we'll make him give you back those strawberries."

Luke looked genuinely surprised by this utterance. He looked across the table at Ryan and asked, "How?"

Matt was ready to leave, and he drove them home. They promised to come back soon. "Good-bye, Grammy and Pop-Pop. See you soon."

I was tired and wanted to take a nap, a recurring habit I'd gotten into. But there was still the repairman working on the auto. "You have to at least keep him company," said Joani. It made no sense. The repairman would rather be left alone. "You could offer him a Pepsi. It's hot out there."

So, I offered him a Pepsi, which he gladly took. I learned a lot about his work today, as he was talkative. It was easy, he said. First, you placed the window where it belonged; then you put glue around it, or something like that. It would hold. Finally, he left. I prepared for a nap. First, I had to hear about Alexandra, who it was determined would stay with us for the night.

After my nap, I felt much better. The girls would be out for a last night of talk-a-thon, including supper. So, after my wife and I had a brief meal, we headed out for frozen yogurt. We ran into some old friends and sat talking until the sun went down; then we headed toward home to see Allyssa, Alexandra, and Katie.

We sat up until midnight. (I'm lucky I got that nap in.) Watching the three girls chow down even more food, we felt blessed. I was ready to start school, my forty-first year, at Harper College on Monday, and nothing was going to get in my way. I signed three books (I had published two novels by then) for the girls, the last time I would ever write with my right hand. Then, we said goodnight and headed for bed. I fell right asleep, sleeping through the night. The morning would change my life.

****

August 17th, 2012. I woke up and stepped out of bed. The sound of my head hitting the bedside table echoed throughout the room. My wife sat up in bed and shouted, "What's the matter, Mike?" I tried to answer, but couldn't. She set me down on the floor. I knew I had had a stroke, and I tried to get up into a sitting position. But try as I might, it couldn't be done. Joani slammed open our door, and I heard her scream, "Girls, get up! Mike's had a stroke, and I need you to write down his prescriptions for his medication."

I started to think what these girls had gone through. Allyssa had her car run through with the neighbor's tree, and Alexandra had her trip to the hospital for a long-range problem. Joani called the neighbors, Mr. and Mrs. Meier, and they came over immediately. Glenn and Kathy were among our best friends, and they had been our neighbors for almost twenty-nine years.

3

Michael J. Bellito

As Kathy rubbed my back, a vision came to me. Several weeks ago in Door County, I had had the symptoms of a stroke. It was one night after dinner as I sat with the others and watched the Olympics on television. Suddenly, I was hit with stroke-like feelings. I got up and walked to the bathroom, without telling any of the others. I stood for the longest time, splashing water on my face. As I walked back to the living room, I was determined not to alarm anyone. Later that night, I told my wife, and she suggested it was because I went swimming for so long with my grandsons. Until that time, it was a stillborn thought.

I remember my trip to the hospital. The paramedics carried me down the stairs and loaded my body into the ambulance. My wife rode in the front, having given Kathy the tough task of calling my son Matt. I looked out the back window, watching the trees go along. A short distance from home, a lady did what she was supposed to do, pulled over her car. And the gentleman behind her, paying no attention, rammed into her. The paramedics made a brief call.

Kathy rang up my son. Matt sat up in bed, wondering who could be calling on his last official day of vacation. When he saw it was Kathy Meier, he knew it couldn't be good. "Hello," he said.

"Hello, Matt, it's Kathy. Your father had a stroke. Your mom's left for the hospital. I think you should go there and be with her. Don't worry yet; your father's a tough man."

Matt hung up the phone. Part of his world had shattered. He said good-bye to his wife Becki and told her not to tell the two boys when they woke up. There would be time for that.

Back at the hospital, Joani told me she was here, which was comforting. I remembered certain things about strokes, that you were paralyzed on one side, meaning you couldn't move your arm or leg. I DIDN'T know you lost your voice, or I would have been screaming in terror. I was, after all, a speech teacher. Suddenly, I realized it was Friday; I had to start my forty-first year of teaching on Monday. Well, I would probably lose a few weeks.

4

I had to have an MRI; this would tell the doctor whether I had the stroke and how serious it was.

Joani said, "He's not suited to the MRI. He's going to freak out in there."

The nurse answered, "We'll give him some medicine. He'll probably fall asleep in there."

Matt arrived. He insisted, although Joani said no, that we call Joy. She was in Ohio, teaching first grade, and married to Stephen. Matt won out; he would call Stephen, who would handle things as he saw fit. Stephen called Debbie, the school's principal, and told her the news. Debbie escorted Joy to the office and told her the news about her father. Joy was three-and-a-half years younger than Matt and eight months pregnant. They made the decision to come to the hospital and arrived around 5:00.

Joani had already learned that it was a major stroke, and that it had caused a blockage in the carotid artery, which meant I was paralyzed on the right side. I could not, of course, speak. She was saddened to learn that I would not receive any intervention medicine. This was a new type of medicine that was meant to dissolve the clot. However, because I didn't know when I had the stroke—since I went to bed at twelve o'clock—they couldn't give me the medicine.

I remember much of the day; my best friends kept on coming. Joani was shocked by a bag that was delivered by Lisa and Mark, a bag carrying everything she'd need in the hospital from snacks to a sweater, one she'd need because hospitals were always cold. Mr. Moon and Denny McSherry came, the former colleague being sure I would die, even though I reached out my hand and grasped his. Rick Wager, my pastor, came and said a prayer. My mom could not be reached. Having spent the day at Lake Geneva, my mom was finally located by Matt, and he delivered the bad news. He went and picked her up, and she joined us at the hospital.

The first few days were mostly involved in sleeping and eating, although the latter was destined to be a calamity because they couldn't tell if I could keep anything solid down. I don't remember anything very well, only the fear that I'd never be able to talk again. My wife admits she was horrified, and she and my daughter went to the block party to tell everyone the news the next night. The neighbors knew; they had already mapped out the Saturdays to cut the grass, rake the leaves, and put away the yard supplies. Joani, on the second or third day, began fearing we would lose the house, the cost of rehabilitation being so high. Becki, who was typing quietly in the corner, spoke up. "There's a cap." Of course, a cap, Joani thought.

There was a nurse that came in with two objects. She asked me which was which, a pen or a banana. I picked the pen as the banana. Oh, boy.

As time wore on, Joani thought less about a problem and more about solutions. She was amazed that they had a speech therapist in the hospital, one who would clearly work with me; one who I did not remember. Joani said I spoke my first complete sentence when I returned from therapy, something I can't recall. This would give me hope. If she only knew how long it would take me.

Matt and Joani left to tour some rehab places. They stopped at the first one, Alexian Brothers Rehabilitation Hospital in Elk Grove. They chose this one over the big place in Chicago. Joani would have a long road, a hard time parking, and traffic to and from the city. This was an easy place to get to, and was in the suburbs.

This was the place they told me I was going. I understood it, as best as I could. We would be leaving tomorrow.

Tomorrow finally came. I had passed the first test; I would be going to rehabilitation. I was no longer on the critical list as I had been moved to a bedroom. At last, I could eat any food I wanted (I thought), and I would not be subject to hearing about McDonald's, Subway, or Wendy's.

I said good-bye to a former student from John Hersey High School (a place I taught), a nurse who had been on patrol since I had moved to the spacious room, and one who asked Joani to please leave the room so she could "check me out," whatever that meant. The two paramedics hoisted me up on the fashionable gurney to take me to Elk Grove. And I was off.

It was Wednesday. Six days had passed, but it seemed like a week. I had journeyed from a healthy individual to a person who was paralyzed on one side and couldn't begin to talk. I had to motorize in a wheelchair. I had gone from an English/speech teacher to one who had to talk just like an infant.

There just wasn't any hope. I knew I had to keep my spirits up, and somehow I did. I seldom ate lunch or dinner alone, so constant were the friends that came to visit. In fact, it was those genuine friends, from church, school, and the neighborhood that kept me alive during that first month.

CHAPTER 2

I was to stay in the Alexian Brothers Rehabilitation Hospital in Elk Grove. I was to stay in my room, complete with a bunk-mate. There was a cafeteria, from which you ordered breakfast, lunch, and dinner. I could only order certain things, which I could be sure to swallow. I remember pointing out the meals I wanted to the nice lady. Joani kept me company at all these meals, which was difficult because I couldn't talk at all, a condition called aphasia.

I was to stay in Alexian Brothers for over five weeks. I was scheduled to show up for occupational therapy, physical therapy, and speech therapy. Only the weekends would be different, a scant few therapists being around. The wheelchair would be my sole source of movement.

The speech therapist was Katie, who was going to get married in October. She talked mostly about my family to see if I could name anybody. It was tough going. She was as nice as can be, and I struggled to name just a few of them. I remember I couldn't pronounce my own wife's name, and she said we better work on that.

I don't remember very much of that therapy, but I remember one thing. I was a writer, and I wanted her to know that. I struggled to say the names: *Ten Again, First Time Around,* and *Abner's Story.* The last one I had sent as a script to a new publisher, and I hoped to hear back soon. That, and the fact that I taught for forty years, impressed Katie. She got me to tell her the stories, and I made some progress before I was dismissed. Some progress was very little progress—I was a speech teacher, and I could say very few words.

Jen was my occupational therapist. She worked with me on lying down and getting up from the bed. Vicky was another occupational therapist. Her finesse was games and puzzles. She gave me seemingly easy puzzles—I had done a 1,500-piece puzzle that was of the Chicago nightline; it was framed. Now, I was facing a 20-piece puzzle. I guessed it through, taking a longer time than I remember. I don't recall the specific games, but I know they seemed hard. We would also work with my arm, stretching it in various ways. All this was done in my wheelchair.

Julie was my physical therapist—I remember the two-wheel bike from her. Veronica was another physical therapist. It was with her that I did my walking. My walk was around the loop, then around the aisles out to the reception desk; I felt like I was accomplishing something. Therapy lasted about fifty minutes, once in the morning and once in the afternoon. By four-thirty, I was done except for dinner and relaxation.

Dinner was never eaten alone. Joani was always in attendance, plus my mother, my brother and his wife, and a few friends. I have to admit, dinner was my favorite—there were tasty tidbits, and I gobbled them down.

Relaxation time was most often spent with Joani. She was into reading the Bible from Moody's *Today in the Word*. This brought me back into the reason I was there: Jesus had a purpose for us to be there. There was something I had to learn from this life-altering change, something I must learn about what I could or should do.

This was the time I asked questions about anything, if I could get them out. The frustration about not being able to talk was mind-bending. I knew what I wanted to say, if I could just say it. That, contained with the stress-inducing need to know everything, left me speechless at times.

This was the time I worried about everything, from the lawn to the sump-pump to whether or not my wife was locking all the doors tightly at night. One night, she came up to the bedroom and looked out the window. There, staring in at her was a raccoon. She shut the windows, and turned on the outside lights at night.

Many an evening was spent looking at the cards I received. There were hundreds, and Joani would read them to me. I have decided to reprint parts or all of them. There are many people that I'm leaving out. Please understand that I'm appreciative of all of them, whether you appear or not. I've kept the lot of them, and I've looked at them many times. Whether they contained Bible verses or not, they were special to me; they helped me back.

Dick and Becky Hill were the most consistent, almost a card a week. One card said: "We can rest easy . . . 'cause the Shepherd never sleeps!!" They added: "Praying for your complete recovery—and soon! Keep working hard." It was a blessing, really, to see all the cards with "keep working hard." It was something I had to keep in mind.

John (an old friend) and Susan Ewalt's card said: "God's love, though never far away, is closer still each time we pray." John added: ". . . especially your positive attitude and determination. Please know you have been in my thoughts and prayers daily and will continue to be so." And then John added: "P.S.—I'd send you a 'Big Man' if I could find one!"—a reference to a childhood game with larger-than-life cowboys.

Brian and Debbie Lantzen, our cousins, wrote this Bible verse:
"But those who wait on the Lord
Shall renew their strength
They will soar on wings like eagles
They will run and not grow weary
They will walk and not be faint."

It was one of the cards that was hung on the blackboard. They wrote: "Joani says you've been claiming that Scripture, and we are praying it for you, too. We hope each day is better than the day before."

Bill and Nancy Feezor wrote: "We heard about Mike last night, so we are very sorry. Our thoughts and our prayers are with him and your whole family." And in the most heartfelt way, considering I always called him the King: "The King commands his Royal Scribe to a speedy recovery. His realm needs him." For twenty-nine years, I knew him as the King. Late one night, a B-B bullet shot through his window, bounced off the closet, and wounded him in the bottom. I always referred to that as the attempted assassination. Long live the King!

Mike and Linda Kozanecki, Door County veterans, wrote: "1 Peter 5:7 says to cast all of your fears and anxiety on Him because He cares for you!" This was the very verse I carried in my wallet the day I had my stroke, and I had carried it in my wallet for twenty-three years. Joani gave it to me in her own script. They ended with: "You are blessed to have so many people to love and support you." I was beginning to realize that.

And even an elderly lady, Norma, who goes to my church said: "I miss you. There is no one that takes care of me like you do. Sending my blessings to you."

My hairdresser, Linda, wrote: "I am so sorry to hear about your stroke! I am happy to come and give you a haircut (don't want you looking like Welcome Back Kotter!)" When she came, they moved her into a bathroom, and she snipped away. Vicki saw me thereafter and said, "Nice haircut, Mike."

Annie Bruce, one of my Speech Team students, wrote: "I'm so sorry to hear about your stroke! My family and I wish you well, and we are praying for your speedy recovery!" And then, in a John Grisham first line from one of his famous novels, she included: "P.S.—The jury was ready." I never laughed so hard.

Annie Marto Timmins said: "The two of you are an amazing couple who have given so much to so many. Now it's time for support and open hearts to come back to you. I am so thankful that God brought you into my life and showed me what a loving couple looks like. I can be a witness." Annie was a part of Joani's work in Teen Mother Choices. Joani mentored her, and we were invited to her wedding.

Rick and Sharon Wager—Rick is my campus pastor, and he was the high-school pastor for my son Matt and my daughter Joy. He also married Matt and Becki. Their card said: "Good news: there's really no such thing as impossible for you, because all things are possible with God. There's no mountain too high, no valley too deep, no trial too wide to stand in His way. He's with you, for you, working on your behalf today. And many who care are praying with you and standing beside

11

you—until we see the impossible come true." Then, they added: "We were so encouraged to hear that you are doing so well spiritually, emotionally, and physically on this difficult journey. We thought it might be fun to 'work on something' with your many visitors!" The 'work on something' was a thousand-piece jigsaw puzzle of Wrigley Field, home of the Cubs. (It turned out to be a masterpiece when I finally did it.)

Ken Ender is the president of Harper College. He sent me a card in which he said: "Art Carlson (a friend from church) has shared the news with me concerning your recent illness. Sounds like you are making progress. Know that Harper College is wishing you well."

And Hersey faculty also wished me well. Bruno Gwardys said: "I have such great memories working with you, Mike; you made a difference in so many people's lives, young and old. You really cared about your students. I will hold you in my prayers and hope that God will get you back on your feet swiftly."

Jack Cutlip sent me a letter. In it, he said: "As you probably know, I have had eight years of doctor visits, many operations, two broken hips, etc. What I would like to share with you, Mike, is for you to keep a positive and cheerful attitude about you in the years ahead. Remember to take baby steps at first, don't become disappointed in yourself if you can't complete a task. Take a step back and see if the goal can be accomplished in another way. Do not dwell on the past, look to the future, and see how you can improve your situation." Well, as I said already, my positive and cheerful attitude has kept me going right from the start.

Dan and Ann Louise Thyreen have a special place in my heart. Dan was my first-year biology instructor at Arlington High School, and he ended up teaching at Hersey. Ann Louise taught second grade to both Matt and Joy. They said: "I now consider it a blessing that we saw you so recently in Door County. We pray for healing, peace, wise doctors, and strength for all of you now and in the weeks to come."

Linda Kleinschmidt, another Door County resident, wrote: "I had just finished reading Mike's second novel and heard about your great family trip to Door County when Koz called with the news about his stroke. You must be as shocked as any of us with plans turned upside down and so much sitting squarely on your shoulders." So much sat directly on Joani's shoulders, and I couldn't get up out of my wheelchair.

I couldn't have expected the one card from Dolores Lindgren, a woman I had not seen for twenty or thirty years. She said: "We were all so fortunate to know and work with each other back in 'those days.' You, Mike, are the one who was able to make us feel such pride by writing your wonderful books. God willing, with good therapy and time, you'll be back to working on your next one within the coming year. (You're so young!) For now, do as you're told and treasure Joani in your life."

Kathy Klaczek, a Wheeling High School teacher, said: "No matter what, you always have a smile on your face. With your awesome attitude, you'll be jogging laps around your neighborhood before you know it!"

Bob and Ann Smith, lifelong friends, wrote in a letter: "We said a prayer at dinner last night for your continued recovery. We have copies of your books here for the kids to read and enjoy. We know you will be writing again soon. Keep the faith—you can do anything you set your mind to. You have the grace and glory of God on your side and the combined strength of all of your family and friends who love you. We believe in you."

Another letter came from Charlie Hess. He said: "We have been thinking of and praying for you, lots, these last days. Like many of the people we've spoken to, our comments were—how could this happen to Mike? He is so young, lively, and mentally engaged. But—life is a gift, and each day is special." He closed with a quote from a "famous" author—the last line of *First Time Around.*

By now, you're probably tired of these, and indeed there are many I've left out. Joani left after we talked about my progress, and I was quite tired by eight o'clock.

Sometime after Joani left, a nurse would come in to give me a shower. These were two times a week; I was used to showers every day. I was still in my wheelchair, and he went over and over my body; it felt so good. I was wheeled out to my bed and helped in. It felt so frustrating to be helped into and out of my bed, but there was nothing I could do.

I was asleep by nine o'clock. I hated to always be on my back, but with my whole right side paralyzed, it was the only way I could get comfortable. I was suddenly awakened by a nurse, who gave me my sleeping pills. I know, wake me up to give me sleeping pills. I was given so many pills, I didn't know what they were. But, I went back to sleep in a hurry.

There was a ninety-three-year-old man in the bed next to mine, and he was a naughty camper. He would mess the bed in the middle of the night, and it would take two of the nurses to change him. I would always wake up.

"Gimme some of dat," he would slur.

"Watch those hands!" a petrified nurse would exclaim.

But, he was suddenly wide awake. His hands would reach out for an ass or a boob, and the sudden shriek from the startled nurse would freeze the room.

They would say, "What is the matter with you? You're too old for that."

"I'm never too old for dat. C'mon, please."

And the rumble would go on for ten minutes or so. I began to appreciate the nurse's duties. Soon, it would all quiet down, and I would fall back asleep.

CHAPTER 3

Jen and Vicky would work with me on sitting up and right-arm exercises. It had been four weeks, and I was convinced I was never going to get out of my wheelchair. I took a nap every chance I got as I was tired every morning. They would let you nap because they knew you were exhausted. The nurses would wake you up to give you pills, and they would start your shift quite early in the morning.

One day, I asked to read a newspaper, the *Chicago Sun-Times*. It was at this juncture that I finally discovered I couldn't read. The draft ran all together. I was reading columns mumbo-jumbo. My heart sank suddenly. All these years of schooling and teaching, and I couldn't even read.

I liked when a friend came to visit at lunch. I could just answer passively, and I didn't have to talk. One day, I was seated at a table with another patient. I had to admit to him that I couldn't even talk. So, I couldn't walk, I couldn't talk or read, and I couldn't even move my right arm, which was in a sling. My right arm meant I had to learn to type and write with my left hand.

Katie made sure I understood what a stroke meant, permanent damage to the brain (not to the leg, the arm, the voice box). There was a chance that I could learn everything, within two to three years, if all went well. With a good deal of therapy, and a whole lot of work, I could learn everything again.

She had me write as much as talk. And then say those things out loud. These were the simplest things. My home address, my phone number, my full name, the names of my wife, my children, my grandchildren. Sometimes I could remember them, sometimes I couldn't. I found the more excited I got, the less I could remember. She had me write out words. I was normally a good speller; this time I wasn't.

Veronica forced me to walk, and I really looked forward to that time. We started out very gradually and built up to a slow gait. I never fell. This was a whole lot better than the time she reprimanded me for going too fast in the wheelchair. I hit only one pole.

I was forced to look at the other people and guess whether they were better or worse than I was. I secretly cheered when I made it past the reception table. I was uplifted when I heard the ladies cheer me on. I was using my hand-walker and my leg brace.

Once a day, I met for a very short time with my doctor, Dr. Marinko. He was my savior (along with my other therapists) because he kept saying I was going to get better. That was my only hope—that better was yet to come.

August rolled into September. Suddenly, it was late September, and I knew what that meant. It meant that I was going to be able to come home, and that Joy would be having her first child. Joani had a decision to make. She had to appeal to the insurance to pick up another five days. First, I was nowhere ready to go home. Second, she would be able to go to Ohio and be with Joy for the delivery of her first baby, something that Joy wanted very much.

While we waited, both Veronica and Jen would escort me to my house and go over things to be sure I was safe. The morning came. I was going to see my home for the first time in over a month, and it seemed like nirvana. As the ladies got me into the Rav4, Joani was going through nervousness. The ride home took twenty minutes, and I felt a shiver going up my spine as we made the final turn onto Kingsport Drive.

The house looked much the same; the trees, the bushes, and all the landscape. I struggled out of the car, and tried to walk. This would be impossible, so they helped me into the wheelchair. Now, came Joani's task. She would have to wheel me up and through the front door. I faced the sky as we rolled up the partition, and I was on my back as we tried to climb up the doorway. I had to hold my breath, but we finally made it up. For the first time in over five weeks, I was in my own home.

I wasn't going to go upstairs or downstairs. I was only going to see the main floor, which included the kitchen, the living room, the dining room, the family room, the laundry room, and the guest bathroom. They made a quick deduction, which was that the toilet needed a metal bar to hoist me up. They were happy that I could reach the items in the refrigerator, and they suggested that we drag down the Lazy-Boy from upstairs to give me something to sit in. Joani would have to bend down and raise the footrest. They studied the stairs and made sure they told Joani she would have to put in a railing on the first ascent; my left hand needed something to grab onto. They looked at the bathroom and showed Joani how to put the shower bench down. Then, they showed her how to operate the hand-held shower, so together we could clean me.

They reminded her I would have to be on the opposite side of the bed, so I could swing off easily. They were generally pleased that I could move my wheelchair with ease around the main part of the house. As we pulled out of the driveway, Veronica and Jen told me to say good-bye to my home, that it would only be another five days or so. We found out when we got back to Elk Grove that the insurance company had granted an extension for me to stay another five days.

A guest speaker was poised to talk about his stroke. Veronica strongly suggested that we did not miss this speaker, so we went. I remember walking into the main venue and seeing a man who looked very much alive and standing on both feet. He could speak regularly. He spoke about having a stroke when he was twenty-seven; he was now forty. He could type with both hands, but his right hand moved slightly; otherwise, he was normal. I was heartened by this man's recovery. If he could do it, maybe so could I.

It was true that generally the older you were, the harder the stroke hit you and the longer it took to overcome the symptoms of it. But, there was something about this man and the way he had never given up. I was encouraged; I would need to be.

17

Veronica looked at the extra five days as a Godsend. She was going to come in on Saturday and Sunday and help me walk and climb those stairs. Also, she made sure that Vicky and Jen gave me showers every day. Other than the fact that I was butt-naked in front of attractive girls, or women, I did just fine.

Walking involved going up and down this staircase many times. When Joani was there, I almost fell. I could see the panic in her eyes. What if this happened when it was just us?

Veronica took us out to the hidden stairwell. Here, she would work me for fifty minutes going first up and then down the staircase. It was panic over ice. I took my time (and that doesn't cut it) going up and down the stairs. The latter was particularly frightening.

****

The phone rang early Monday morning. It was Joani. Joy's water bag had broken; it was time. Joani would leave immediately for Oxford, a five-hour drive. She was calling me to let me know I would not see her today, and I would be all right. Sure, I would be all right, as long as I didn't think about her driving all alone without me. I had always driven all the way on vacation or otherwise. She had only taken the wheel when I had not been there. Well, I was not there this time.

She arrived at the hospital at around 4:00. Stephen checked in with her by shouting, "She's pushing! The baby is almost here! I gotta go back now!" Charlotte, a baby girl, was born around 4:30. Joani had made it just in time; God was watching over the whole thing.

Joani was ushered into the delivery room to see Joy and Charlotte. It was the one thing that Joy wanted. Both women smiled like crazy when they held the baby. I had been there for the birth of Luke and Ryan; I was going to miss this one.

I received the call from Joani later that night. It was a little girl, named Charlotte, born Monday, September 24th, 2012. She told me she would be back on Wednesday with plenty of pictures to show me, and she promised she would drive safely.

One thing was wrong with that task; she talked to Joy early Tuesday morning and decided to leave. Stephen and Joy were bonding as most parents did, and she didn't want to interrupt their solitude. Besides, she thought, it was me she had to get home to.

Joani arrived sometime in the late afternoon. I was surprised, to say the least, and overjoyed to see her. She showed me, and everyone else, the pictures of baby Charlotte. I was pleased as punch to be a grandfather for the third time, and I let everyone know it.

We had dinner together, the second-to-last one. Tomorrow would be my last day at Elk Grove. I thought how much I had gained, and how much I had yet to learn. The plan would be to let at-home assistants in to help me talk and do certain things around the house. The key was I was supposed to learn to do everything I could to help Joani. Most would take a year; some would take longer.

I could read. That was a fact. It had taken me about five weeks to get it down, and I still realized I had to slow down and grasp the material. But it was becoming easier. That was a blessing.

And there was the letter from the publisher. "Dear Michael: We would be happy to publish *Abner's Story* at Oak Tree Press. You have thirty days to respond to this letter. We would love to have you."

Joani received the query just after I was in the rehabilitation center, but she hid it from me until near the end. "Well, what do you think? Matt and I both think you should be honest. That's the only way you can do it. Let her know about your stroke, and then the decision will be what it is."

She was right. It hurt like hell to leave it up to some publisher, but that was the right decision. She sent the note; I was a stroke victim, and there was no two ways about it.

Wednesday went quickly. Thursday, September 27th, 2012, arrived. It was my son Matt's thirty-third birthday, and I was going home. I woke up long before the nurses came to get me up.

"Well, you're going home," they said. Nothing would sound sweeter in my life.

Joani and I picked out gifts for the five therapists and the doctor: copies of *Ten Again* and *First Time Around.* They weren't autographed; I hadn't reached that point with my left hand yet.

Veronica and Jen walked us to the car. They gave us last minute instructions about how to "take it easy" and "don't give up." We were at home by 11:30. The hardest part was yet to come.

CHAPTER 4

"Well, we're off to church," I stated.

"No, I don't think so. We'll wait until next week. See how things go," Joani said.

To tell the truth, I was just glad to be home. I had until Monday, October 1st, before the OT, PT, and ST would show up and put me to work. Joani had the family room redecorated. She had the men from church move the Lazy-Boy chair downstairs so I could sit in it. They had put in the metal bar for the toilet and the new railing on the stairwell so I could have something to grip on.

Most of the day, I sat in my wheelchair with my right leg and my right armrest on. I took a fairly long nap in the afternoon. I was ready for bed at nine o'clock.

I'll be honest. I don't remember much of what was said or done during this period. I guess Joani tried to let me talk as much as possible, but that was few and far between. I shimmied up the stairs, going one step at a time; I was asleep by nine-fifteen. I had to get up about four to five times a night, but there was no way I was going to put my shoes on and hold the pee in. So, I woke up Joani and called to her; she had to hurry over to my side of the bed, and hold the glass bottle, and I'd urinate in it. I don't know how many months that went on, but it was at least six months.

The next movement was to bathe and dress. The most I remember about this is how long it took at first, then how we eventually cut it down. I sat on the shower bench, lugging my right leg in last. I washed myself down, using Coast liquid soap; then Joani hosed me down using the hand-held shower. I must admit, all the time I was using this, I felt cleaner than I ever did before. Joani applied the shampoo, and rinsed it down. I was clean; all I had to do was dry up. I held my right arm up; she put on the deodorant. It was late September, so it was still appropriate to wear t-shirts and shorts. Joani let me try my best to put on the outerwear. The hardest part was the socks and shoes, mainly because my feet were semi-wet.

Next would involve Kathy, the next-door neighbor. It was about 8:30 when she'd come over every day for the first three weeks. I had to go down the stairs, and allow me to say, it was slow at best. With Joani on my backside and Kathy on my front, I managed to make it down. It should be said that I never fell on the way down.

I could now relax and eat my breakfast. There were five pills before breakfast and two pills after supper. They were all easy to swallow, and therefore I never minded taking them. Then, I would go to the bathroom and shave and brush my teeth. The brushing of my teeth was accomplished with an electric toothbrush; the shaving was done with my electric razor.

The next day, Saturday, was a celebration for my son Matt's birthday. Luke and Ryan had seen me once already, so they were prepared for what they might see. My biggest loss was not being able to play with them in the yard. I thought back to our vacation in Door County a couple of weeks before my stroke. The men all built a giant sand castle, and there's a cool picture of it hanging on my refrigerator. We had a good time, but they were only three, so they had a hard time understanding my wheelchair and the fact I couldn't talk.

I don't remember much about my home care. The lady who was my physical therapist worked me super hard, especially in the things I didn't like. I abhorred the stairs, so up and down we went. She stuck right with me, so I didn't fall, and she did build my confidence.

My occupational therapist concentrated on what I ate for meals and my handwriting with my left hand. She would write out some gobbledy-gook, and have me copy it. I didn't notice it then, but my handwriting was slowly getting better. She said it was best to drink eight glasses of water per day (and no pop). Yeah, and then I'd really have to go to the bathroom.

The man who was my speech therapist really worked me hard, and he left homework for me to do. He was the nicest man, but he knew what he was doing. I was hesitant with certain sounds, and he hit on those. A long list of material that started with "s" or ended with "th" was where he started.

I did my exercises all the time, and I kept up with my speech therapy. But my laziness was beginning to show, and Joani couldn't wait for me to go to therapy five days a week. It was easy for me to sit and watch television (I still didn't know how to work the remote) or read a book (something I was barely recovered at). After one week of therapy, it was time to attend church.

What was a big event for me turned out to be hell for Joani. She had to make sure we got up an hour early, she had my clothes laid out, and she had to get my wheelchair ready to go. We shot back and forth at each other like snakes in a battle, but we were ready to go on time. We used my cane to get me down the steps in the garage and into the car. Then, she lugged my wheelchair into the trunk, a particularly hard task for her.

For a long time, I had to get used to Joani driving, and I was relatively easy on her, something I was not accustomed to. Then, the church approached. I had not seen it through half of August and all of September. Would the people shy away from me?

Joani sat me down on a chair in the vestibule; she went out to get the wheelchair. I looked around. Suddenly, I was surrounded with women. With tear-stained eyes and kisses galore, they smooched me. I was in heaven. I did not know, up until that time, how much everyone cared in the church. I felt like crying, but I was too stunned.

We sat in the back, unlike the front seats we usually sat in. Pastor Rick Wager came and said hello. During his talk before the sermon, he drew the attention of everyone to my presence there. "It is my privilege to announce that Mike is back with us today."

All the church turned and looked at me; there was applause. You could have carried me out that day. I felt so good. As the weeks went past, we abandoned my wheelchair and moved up to the front, but I'm getting ahead of myself.

Back at home, we continued to work with the therapists, and I sensed it was time to move on. Joani, in particular, felt trapped by my presence. She could never leave home. She tried to get me to do things by myself; I just wanted to be lazy and sit around. My grandsons came with Matt to help Joani rake the leaves. As they worked together in the front yard, I was content to sit by the front door in my wheelchair and just watch. It was at moments like this that I felt helpless and ashamed, knowing that I could never rake the leaves or cut the grass or blow the snow away, things I loved to do.

Before October 22nd, the day I was supposed to register for therapy, I got a little careless. I ignored my wife, and steered my wheelchair toward the bathroom; I was going to get up and use the restroom. But I'd forgotten to lock my brakes.

I rose suddenly and felt the wheelchair slip. I was falling to my right, onto the hard tile floor. I let out a gag and grabbed for anything I could—the handle of the basement stairs. It slowed the impact down a bit, but not enough. I landed hard, my breath knocked out of me. The next thing I heard was my wife scream.

Joani ran to me. I tried to assure her I was okay, but my body felt otherwise. She called my neighbor Glenn to help me get up, which he did; I was helpless. The next morning, we would see. Upon waking up, I was stiff and sore on both elbows, both knees, and with a pain around the chest. I had not broken any bones. It was the only time I fell on my own.

Sometime during those weeks, I received a note from the publisher. It read: "We are so sorry to hear about Mike's stroke. Tell him we will publish his story whenever he's ready to do the editing—in other words, whenever he's ready. We love the story."

I was ecstatic. I had Joani call up my editor Erin Brooks. She was to come by my house and take my manuscript for editing. Erin came over the next day and took my novel away.

Erin was the best editor in the world. She read every page and marked what needed to be changed or what might—as long as I saw fit—be changed. When she came back, she left me with red-inked pages.

Alone at night, I thought about Wheeling RIC until I went to sleep, usually not a long time. It was very close to my house. In fact, it was only five minutes away, a true blessing. I would get up at 6:30, bathe and dress by 7:00, and then go downstairs. I would eat a hearty breakfast—a banana and some cereal with fruit on it, milk and orange juice to drink—go to the bathroom and shave and brush my teeth. Then, we would be off and running by 8:10.

My schedule would be 8:30 to 11:20, fifty minutes of speech therapy, occupational therapy, and physical therapy, only a half-day to start with. I would spend the second half of the day sleeping on my Lazy-Boy, a good two-hour nap to begin with. Then, I would just laze around the house, always in my wheelchair.

I was terrified to go the first day. I didn't know what I would do or whom I would meet. Joani had to have me there by 8:00 because there would be forms to fill out. I climbed out of the car and perched in my wheelchair. The Wheeling RIC was a relatively small place, from what I could see. The first person I met was the friendly John, who had me fill out a bunch of forms. I was not yet proficient with my left hand, so Joani did all of the signing, except where my name was needed.

I was done with all the forms, and now we wheeled back to meet with one of the first occupational therapists I saw. She guided me through a series of questions, none of which I can remember now. Joani said good-bye; and I was wheeled past the kitchen and into the room that was used for sitting from 9:20-9:30 and from 10:20-10:30.

I said "hi" to a woman, and she tried to engage me in conversation for ten minutes. I looked around. Besides the two big tables, there was a rack with all types of medicine balls, a series of mats, and a bunch of beams. Besides that, there was a closet full of games, and a bar full of hand holders. There was an exercise bike, and some steps going up. I had entered the most fabulous place, but I didn't know it at the time.

25

CHAPTER 5

The woman looked at the work sheet. "Ooooh, you got Kyle for PT. Don't worry. I have him too. He's a lot scarier when you first meet him."

I wasn't worried—until now.

The bell didn't ring, but tons of people came scurrying into the room. A tall, thin gentleman came over to meet me. "Hi. I'm Kyle."

We shook hands briefly.

"Don't bring your wheelchair. Leave it at home. Your wife will really like that."

"What?"

"You heard me."

This was unbelievable. He really was nasty. "Kyle the mean man" was who he'd be forever more. I wanted to go home.

He went over some basic questions, and then he told me to do certain things—like sit on the chair and turn around slowly. He took me out to the main hall and told me to move as fast as I could—without hurting myself—down to the end and then come back. I struggled to do that three times. Then, he took me back to the main door that led into the room.

"All right. Here's what you're going to do. This path leads around past the checkout desk, down the main hall, through the dining room off of the kitchen, and through the room. I want you to move as fast as you can—without hurting yourself—and I'll time you."

"How long?"

"Six minutes."

"Six?"

"Look, don't try and kill yourself. We'll do this every two weeks or so, and we'll see how you improve. Okay, get set."

I "set" as well as I could, and we were off. I walked the way I always walked, with my right knee straight. I kicked that out and landed with my right foot. I walked rather fast until the last two laps, and then I was dead.

Kyle kept yelling, "Move it! You can walk faster!" And they said he wasn't cruel.

As I finally reached the main door, I felt like I was going to collapse. I breathed deeply and rested my hand on the wall.

"Would you like some water?"

Was this another test to see how really weak I was? I couldn't talk; I just nodded my head "yes." Kyle disappeared. He returned a moment later with the coolest glass of water I had ever tasted.

"You did well, Mike. You can go back and sit down. It's just about break time."

I went back, found my wheelchair, and sat back down. Rivulets of sweat kept cascading down my forehead. I was spent. It had been over two months since I'd had a workout like that, and I was really feeling it. The nice woman started up right away. "You had Kyle. He's really scary at first."

I couldn't talk; I just nodded. I thought about Kyle. He was easily taller than I was, 6 ft., 3 in. He had brown hair, and dressed in neat clothes with fashionable shoes. (I found out that he always sported a tie on Tuesdays. It was "tie Tuesdays.") He didn't talk much. I found out that was because I couldn't answer him.

Next, I went to a nice speech therapist. I discovered I'd seen her before, at Alexian Brothers Rehabilitation Hospital in Elk Grove. She told me she subbed for some people. She took me through some basic reading, making sure to correct me if I ever did wrong. When it was time to go, she told me I was going to be split up between two ladies. Kristina was the main one, who was out on vacation. She was described as being mean when I first got to know her. Oh, great, that's just what I needed. A petulant PT and stubborn ST. Well, I was certainly ready to meet my OT tomorrow. Perhaps she'd make me hold up my right arm until it fell off.

Joani picked me up. I was too tired to tell her much of anything. She was happy Kyle told me to leave the wheelchair at home. I slept away the afternoon.

The next morning, I met with my OT. Her name was Sue, and she was one of the nicest people I'd ever met. She went over the list with me, and it seemed like she was the best at-home therapist I would ever need. She would teach me to vacuum, dust, cook, work in the yard, and dress myself. She would also allow me to play games, some of which I got really good at. And she would help me to stretch out my arm, so it wouldn't become all numb and stuck to my side. She told me she only worked on Tuesdays, Wednesdays, and Thursdays, so I would have somebody else on the other days.

I met with Kyle also, who was really mean. He forced me and two other guys over to the bars and made us do all sorts of pointless exercises. I found out he hated Notre Dame and the Cubs, and he golfed his afternoons away; oh, and he liked country-western music. I spoke up—what little I could—and reminded him that the Irish had an undefeated record, and he just laughed and told me to continue to do my exercises. He also told us he was twenty-seven and was engaged to be married. Poor girl.

During the breaks, I got to meet some of the patients, of whom there were many kinds. There were stroke, burn, and broken limbs victims. One guy, who was a freshman at ISU, was involved in a party when the police crashed into it. He thought the quickest way out was to climb out the window. It was a fourth-floor window. He landed, with force, body down; the lucky thing was he wasn't paralyzed. The unlucky thing was he broke both his arms and his legs. He was in therapy for over a year, and that didn't count all the operations he had. He was in good spirits.

Another guy was just a half-block from home, riding with two friends, none of whom were drunk. Some woman ran over the median strip and killed his two friends. She was drunk; she lived. He was smashed up rather bad. In spite of the multiple operations, he was walking around, smiling. He told me he

28

wasn't always in good spirits. When he was down at Chicago, he yelled and bit regularly until he realized he was this way, and nothing was going to make it better. It was at times like this that I took a good look at myself and thought that I had been lucky. I was still alive and only good things awaited me.

A guy, who was much younger than I, was out horseback riding with his wife. They hit a small stream, and his horse would not go across. He stepped over the stream and pulled at the horse. He looked down for a minute, and the horse charged forward, ramming into him. He lay paralyzed on the ground while his wife rode for help. He said he knew it was bad when a helicopter whisked him away to the nearest hospital. He walked hesitantly, and his hands were all bunched up. He had girls who were still in high school, and his family had to buy a ranch house so he could get around. He had been in a type of therapy for two years, and he was making some progress. He was always smiling.

****

Halloween. It only came once a year. The little monsters would go out and fill their bags with all the candy they could get. In the olden days, our neighborhood was filled with children. Joani and I would go through fifteen bags of candy—easy. But, as I said before, we'd been living in this house for close to twenty-nine years. (In fact, the house was the first one on the block.) The kids had all grown up—some had married and had kids of their own—and moved out. The last years hadn't been as productive as the first twenty-five or so, but I'd found a way to keep all this candy for me.

I was gorilla-man. I wore a sweatshirt, black in color, inside out. I fitted my hands with gorilla-gloves, the sharp nails protruding from the black, hairy fingers. The mask was to die for, literally. It looked like King Kong. The teeth were razor-like. The hair could be teased into an Afro. And the best part was two red eyeballs that blinked when I turned on the battery. I would scare any kid from here to Alaska. So, I sat on the wooden bench on the front porch of my house, a pumpkin full of delicious candy waiting for the kids—if they dared.

There were two kinds of children: one that travels by himself, that doesn't allow other children to slow him down with idle conversation. He was always the first one. One kid, moving rather quickly, high-tailed it up to the porch, saw me sitting there, turned around and shuffled away. Like I said, he wasn't going to let anybody slow him down.

The other type of children came in one big group. They probably wasted an hour waiting for a kid. They'd come up to the porch, see me sitting there, and freeze. There was always dialogue.

"He's alive!" the brightest one shouted.

"No, he's not. He's only a stuffed gorilla, and he's holding the candy!"

"Well, I'm not going up."

(By now, nightfall had come, and they had to go home.)

Finally, one of them seemed braver than the rest. "Well, if you're such a chicken, I'm going up!"

I never had to move. I only extended one finger upward, and that did it. Several shrieks followed by mass panic as they ran each other over.

One time, my daughter Joy was standing out on the sidewalk with a couple of her friends when a lonesome ghost came up to the porch.

"Hey, Dad. Don't scare him. It's Bhumi's brother."

All right. I won't scare him. C'mon, here. Take some candy from my hand. Here's a nice Butterfinger.

He reached out slowly, and took the candy.

As he walked away, he did two things that were quite naughty. Number one: he walked on the grass. Number two: he kept looking back at me. I would have ignored the walk on the grass. I mean, it was Halloween, and kids did stupid things. But, for some reason, the turning around staring at me, as if I was going to get up and chase him, irritated me. If you look at me one more time . . .

30

He did it. I flew off the bench and came flying at the helpless kid. He turned and ran. As he hit the sidewalk, he tripped on his ghost costume. Down he went, the blood spilling from his head. I was fearful of a lawsuit; I tried to bribe him with some extra candy. My daughter Joy looked at me as if I was the last person she wanted to see right now.

Another time, Patty had donned her kids with special homemade costumes, the entire Mickey and Minnie family. They went to about four houses, and then Michelle and Matt saw me. "I'm done. We go home."

This year, I sat in my wheelchair, watching what few children there were scamper past the house. One kid pointed at the bench and wondered where gorilla-man was. I'm still here, kid.

CHAPTER 6

M y wife Joani had to go to work on Wednesday evening. She worked for TMC—Teen Mother Choices. This was an organization that had been around for almost twenty years. It helped teenaged girls, who had chosen to have and raise their babies, develop life skills. There was one mentor to be paired with every girl, some adult woman who was in the act of raising her children, who trained the girls socially, financially, and spiritually. The girls were forced to attend on Wednesday night, where they would have a sit-down meal—provided by a volunteer and something the girls didn't have at home—and an hour of a guest speaker, a financial counselor or someone who would provide the girls with a craft or something to bake. They were also required to get grades that were not below a "C", and not get pregnant again while they were in the program. Since most husbands had left the girls, the program would give them something to lean on, including money for day care.

My wife had to quit her job or find a replacement for me on Wednesday night. She found two—my mom and Mr. Moon. My mom would come about three o'clock and would play games with me. Mr. Moon would come when my mom left and would fix dinner for me—my wife had already warmed it up in the crock pot. I was allowed to sit at the table—I was not allowed to be anywhere near the making of the meal. It was like having Kyle in the kitchen.

Mr. Moon would feast out on certain meals—pot roast, sloppy joes, and hamburger soup. In fact, he liked just about everything. But—and he said this was the reason he came—there were leftover (from Halloween) Reese's chocolate and peanut butter cups. In the freezer, of course.

He would clean the kitchen like it had never been cleaned before, turn my Cubs' logo upside down on the refrigerator, and lead me into the family room where we would watch TV. He would fall asleep often, but when the Blackhawks were on, he usually stayed awake.

Mr. Moon became my best friend then. He stuck with me all winter long, and made me laugh so many times—and so hard—I couldn't believe it. And there was one time of sadness, where I turned to him and said I felt like I was going to be this way forever. He jumped on me and told me to cut it out, that there was plenty of time to get well, and that's what I was going to do.

"That's what I was going to do" took place at the Wheeling RIC. Kristina was every bit as mean at first. She even assigned homework to me because she sensed I wasn't doing anything at home. She had the gall to tell me I wasn't going to do much because my need to talk wasn't as great as when I was with her—in other words, I didn't try to make social conversation. Why, of all the nerve! I didn't realize then that she had my best interests at heart, and it wasn't long before I'd see what a wonderful woman she was.

The other woman, Sarah, was a bit nicer. She didn't always have me verbalize. She knew, if I wanted to be a writer, I was going to have to type again, and that was with my left hand if my right hand didn't work. So, she set about letting me type with my left hand on a story of my own making.

She said, "Where do you like to travel?"

I answered, "We go to Dis- Disney World."

"Then, write about that. Tell me the three rides you like to go on."

Well, fifty minutes wasn't near enough. First, I had to think of those ideas. Next, I had to type up the ideas. Sarah said, "Take your time. If you don't finish it today, you can do it the next time we meet."

The final product wasn't much for as long as I typed. Still, I was somehow proud of it. I mean, it was my own creation and it was done (finally). Sarah posted it on the cafeteria bulletin board, so everyone could read it.

33

It read: "Disney World opened on October 1ˢᵗ, 1971. It was hosted by Roy Disney (Walt's brother) and Mickey Mouse. It only had the Magic Kingdom and two hotels, the Contemporary and the Polynesian. Today, it has four major theme parks and two water parks, plus over twenty-five hotels. My family (Matt, Joy, Joani, and I) made trips down there once every two summers. Our favorite rides were: Big Thunder Mountain Railroad, Splash Mountain, and the Jungle Safari.

"Big Thunder Mountain Railroad is a twisting, turning roller coaster ride that churns a passenger along. The line is long, but the wait is worth it—unless the patron has had too much food. Once, I saw one of my high school students in line, and he asked (in surprise), 'What are you doing here?' I responded, 'I'm sentenced to watch you.' He believed me.

"Splash Mountain is one of the neatest, and wettest, rides in the entire park. A passenger is enjoying the scenery for about ten minutes, going up slowly, so one's not aware of it. Then, one scary moment later, the guest is hurtling downward while being sprayed—or splashed—with water. The poor souls that survive the ride are doused with water from head to foot.

"The Jungle Safari is one of the original rides from Disneyland, created in 1955. It is one of the most interesting rides in the park. Guests are seated in a long, narrow boat that makes its way through the jungles of Africa, not knowing what is going to happen next. The tour guide offers some advice, mostly tongue-in-cheek. All in all, everyone survives.

"Those are the three major rides that my family enjoys the most. Disney World is a magical place that every kid—or adult—should experience."

****

Sue met with me, and after stretching my arm out for fifteen minutes, said, "Let's go to the kitchen."

There, she coaxed me into admitting I didn't do much preparing in the kitchen. Except for the occasional salad or soup, I hadn't made a dinner to speak of. She said we'd start with something I could handle and everybody loves—chocolate chip cookies.

The hardest part of the task was making everything with one hand, my awkward left hand, especially the stirring. But, in the end, I got everything out, mixed it together, and made the best batch of chocolate chip cookies that man or woman had ever tasted. Even Kyle, who swore by them, ate three or four.

Speaking of Kyle, he became meaner than ever when he introduced me to the treadmill. This, he told me, would be my passion three times a week. He said it would help me strengthen my right leg. He was right. I hated it to no avail, especially at first. He would spend about ten minutes harnessing me up to a brace, so I wouldn't fall out. However, I might crack my skull open on the machinery. Oh, splendid.

One day, he got it going rapidly, I lost my balance and flew outward and back. The noise was horrendous.

Kyle said, "Wow, it's never done that before."

He thought about it and decided to do something. He fixed it by turning the machine inside out. The bulk of the machine was behind me, so I couldn't hit my head. Ironically, this worked. It made me not afraid of getting on the treadmill. As the months passed by, I even looked forward to the treadmill because it made me stronger and, therefore, I ran faster in the six-minute run.

One time, when I was completely delirious, I asked Kyle to put the number up high, so I could beat everybody. I beat everybody, all right. I even posted the number with the time. But, I couldn't move my left leg for over a week; the IT band was stretched out, and it took Kyle some rubbing with his stick to make it right. I screamed, much to his delight.

"Well," mused Kyle, "we won't pull that stunt again."

In fact, it only lasted one day. When the guy who had been injured by the horse beat me by a margin, I wanted another chance.

Kyle said, "Not in this lifetime."

He did have some sense. When he had two or three guys, he usually had them spread out on the bar to do exercises. To make this fun, he often grabbed the business section of the *Tribune* and turned to the "This Happened on This Date." He quizzed us, and the first one to get the answer right would get his "good answer." There were no prizes; no gifts. I was struggling remembering names and direct objects—an English teacher, no doubt. I would see the person's visage in my mind, but no answer would pop into my head.

Kyle said, "With this election in 1960, we chose the second— that's the second—youngest man ever to be our president. Who was it?"

I would see John F. Kennedy's face, but would not be able to say his name until it was too late. Needless to say, I never got any "good answers" from Kyle.

At the middle of November, Kyle informed me that we could add some days to my calendar.

"How would you like to add two more full-time days to your schedule? Say Tuesday and Thursday?"

My wife was clearly in favor; I was not.

Therefore, starting sometime in late November, I was onto a partial full-time schedule. Tuesday and Thursday, I would meet twice with an OT, PT, and ST. It went from 8:30 to 3:00; I slept most of those nights.

When I wasn't sleeping, I was trying to watch television, with little luck. It was evident my glasses weren't allowing me to see as they should be. I'd found out that unclear vision is sometimes a possibility after a stroke. I dreaded a trip to find out the truth—my vision was forever ruined.

Dr. Thoms was very nice, and she told me the truth. My vision was only temporarily interrupted by the stroke. Two sets of new glasses (one regular; one sunglasses) did the trick. I could see again. If only the other symptoms of the stroke could vanish as quickly.

CHAPTER 7

Thanksgiving was approaching. Finally. I would have four days with no therapy. As usual, it was Kyle who told me the way it was.

"You have to come to work on Friday."

"What?" I mumbled, almost slipping on the treadmill.

"Watch it," Kyle said. "You almost fell. Christmas is the same way—the 25th is all we get off; and the 1st for New Year's Day."

I picked up speed. I quietly fumed as I thought about it. All my life, I had had the Friday after Thanksgiving (and the day after Christmas off). Well, I'd ask Joani about playing hooky, but I might as well ask the Sheriff of Nottingham for a tax break.

"You were a teacher, right? Well, we work a full week." Kyle sniggered.

Well, I thought, at least I'd only have a half-day.

My daughter Joy, her husband Stephen, and new daughter Charlotte would be spending Thanksgiving in Pennsylvania. Therefore, we would be going to Matt's house to celebrate the day with Becki's parents and siblings. Joani suggested I bring my wheelchair; there would be many people there, including young children running around, and I would feel safer in my wheelchair.

It was the first time I'd be out in public. We had a close relationship with Becki's parents—Wade and Darlene—so I wouldn't feel awkward.

It was Matt's and Becki's first Thanksgiving, and it was a great success. I was only out of my wheelchair for trips to the bathroom. However, there was a touch of sadness—Luke and Ryan, those twins, hardly spoke to me. They played by themselves for the most part. The frustrating thing about the whole situation was my lack of mobility. I couldn't talk and I couldn't walk—what good was I?

The Sunday after Thanksgiving it was time to put up the Christmas decorations—with help. Joani made a nice dinner for Glenn and Kathy, Emil and Patty, and Bob and Lori. All they had to do was go down into the basement and bring up the heavy boxes. Once up, they had to set up the Christmas tree and—most importantly—the Christmas village. I was sans wheelchair to make a better impression. I limped around while the neighbors did all the work.

The Christmas tree was beautiful. It had the multi-colored lights on it already—over 1,400. The ornaments went on with the speed of light. I had sworn to Joani that I'd let the neighbors do the hard work, and the truth was I couldn't keep up. Kathy, Patty, and Lori put the ornaments—all in spaced-out positions— before I could work up the nerve to tell them they were all wacky. Well, I certainly wouldn't allow that to happen with the Christmas village.

Patty took charge. She opened the box with the village houses, trees, people, and snow. Whenever I got nervous, I'd only be able to say one word—"No!" So, as Kathy and Patty tried to put up the village in record time, I babbled "No! No! No! No!" I fell to my knees, and stopped the two ladies in their tracks. I was lucky the box was there to hold me up; otherwise, I would have fallen face forward onto the carpet. Joani was clearly angry, but nothing would stop me now.

"No! No! No! This goes here!" I bellowed. I was taking Christmas back. I may have needed help, but I didn't need interference. Finally, from left to right: the lighthouse, the school building, the gazebo, the toy shop (with Santa out in front), the church, and the antique store. Gramma Green's ole Christmas tree beamed from the right side. There were big trees all around it, and a man and his children brought their Christmas tree home on a sled to decorate. There was the couple drawn against the wind coming out of the antique store. There was the fence with the gate out in front of the church; the nativity was nestled up in one of the crevices with the girl holding the dog looking at it. A duo played their songs by the gazebo. A bunch of children built a snowman by the Heritage sign. A snow sleigh barreled along by the lighthouse. The Christmas village looked perfect.

Joani said she would take care of the rest of the decorations; it was time for dinner. The hamburger soup tasted very good, and the neighbors left knowing that they had been there when I took charge of the village.

When I was back at RIC, I was going to go out—to Abt to Costco and to Barnes and Noble. It was now early December, and it would prove to be one of the mildest winters, a blessing for Joani and me. We had the bath down to a whirl, and the short ride, without any snowstorm, was a pleasure to take. I was always there at 8:20, sometimes even earlier. I saw my name on the calendar for Abt, an electronics store. I would have to ask Kyle what it meant.

He had me struggling as he stretched me out. "We have to make sure you're firm and in shape. Otherwise, the treadmill will eat you alive." Kyle laughed.

"I don't care." The treadmill didn't scare me as it once did.

Kyle frowned.

"I see my name on Friday as going to the Abt store. What does this mean?" I mumbled.

"Well, the administration feels that you should be out and about. So, we'll take you out to some big store, and let you feel your way around."

It sounded great. Better than those exercises on the long bar.

Friday came and went. I asked Kyle about it. He said we postponed it until Monday.

"What?"

Kyle was matter-of-fact. "Don't worry. You'll get out there."

Monday featured a fifty-minute warm up of exercises. Kyle announced at the break, "Okay. Use the bathroom. We're going to Abt."

Finally. We loaded into the van, five of us plus two therapists. I couldn't quite make it; my right leg didn't slide into the van. Kyle lifted it and pushed it into the van.

Michael J. Bellito

It felt good to be out of rehabilitation. Come to think about it, this was the first time I'd been out to any store. Half of August and all of September through November, I'd been cooped up in therapy facilities. You have to think what that meant to me. Here was a guy who was used to driving his own car going wherever he pleased. Now, he was a passenger trapped in a van filled with people like myself with a nutcase driving.

Kyle pulled into Abt. "Well, we're here. You have about an hour to fill out this form."

Oh, great. They couldn't have you just relax and browse through the biggest electronics store in the area. They had to make sure you were on task.

Kyle split everyone up. Those who could walk were by themselves. I was paired up with—guess who? We stood in Abt's large entryway and looked at the store. Kyle showed me the form, and it looked like we would have to travel the width and breadth of the store. Also, we would have to ask one of the store clerks for answers. I hated to talk. But, that was the reason for doing it.

I'll admit, Kyle was with me all the way. He forced me to ask for help when I didn't know which way to go. He forced me to search out every washing machine and dryer to find the very best buy. He allowed me to sit and rest when I was tired, but there was no way he was going to force me up the escalator.

"No way," I stated.

"C'mon. It'll be easy. You can do it. All you have to do is put one foot on the moving escalator, then put the other foot on."

And what if the other foot chose not to move? Then I'd be in hot water, wouldn't I?

I geared up, but in the end, I wouldn't do it.

I'll give Kyle some credit here; he didn't force me to risk life and limb. He simply said, "Some other time."

He turned out to be a prince of a guy when he pulled the van into Dairy Queen before going back to RIC. I ordered a small ice cream cone, and Kyle paid for it. It was a nice thing to do. Maybe he wasn't such a jerk, after all.

Next up, Costco. Kyle went back to making me push around one of those carts. He said it gave me better balance. I struggled around the big store looking for items we needed in the kitchen: milk, bread, fruit, and some candy. I was familiar with Costco because I shopped there with my wife. Kyle was impressed. He bought me another Coke at the exit, and we waited for the rest of the party to join us.

Just before Christmas, we hit up Barnes and Noble. This was my chance to show them what I'd done. Kyle was supposedly my leader, but there was one time I looked up, and he was over in another section of the store. Finally, he came to me, and I was able to lead him to the fiction section.

"Come over here." I led him to my section, and I pulled out the two books that I'd written: *Ten Again* and *First Time Around*. (*Abner's Story* would come later.)

Kyle said, "You wrote these? By yourself?"

"Yep," I said.

Kyle was blown away. Well, not blown away. He didn't buy one. He said, "I'll buy one the next time I'm in here."

****

Christmas came along on the 25th, same time as always. Joy and Stephen were here from Ohio with our new little granddaughter Charlotte. We went to church on Christmas Eve, sat down in front like we had always done in the past. I thought, here I am, in church on Christmas, and I felt like I always had, thankful. Little did I know, I was just beginning what was to be a long and sometimes painful journey. Considering I couldn't talk yet, a silent journey.

Christmas day included Joani's mom Alice and her good friend Elmer, my mom Dolores, Matt and Becki with their twins Luke and Ryan, and Joy and Stephen and Charlotte. We sat in the living room to open presents. The children gave us a new television set (what a surprise!), and everyone sat at the dining room table to eat the ham, potatoes, vegetables, and salad. We finished the day with Joy's homemade pumpkin pie. (Kyle had promised me we would not do the treadmill.)

Late in the evening, I sat in the living room and watched the twins, dressed in their Christmas pajamas, wrestle with themselves. I had the Lord to thank for my so-far remarkable recovery. What 2013 would bring!

CHAPTER 8

As we approached January, I was told the day before Good Friday would be my last day. I worked hard to pass my goals. I already liked Sue, and I was beginning to like Kristina and even Kyle.

Kristina pulled me over to learn to talk into the machine (I don't remember the name) that types what you say. I started with, "My name is Mike." It typed out, "My game is Bike." Oh, splendid. We worked on that for about a month, and it was determined that my speaking was far too mumbled to come up with a sentence that made sense. I was dismissed. Imagine—a speech teacher not being able to come up with a simple sentence. Kristina told me to keep working on it, and maybe we would try it later.

Kyle became convinced that the treadmill was the answer to all my problems. If not the treadmill, then the bike. He would sit me down on the bike that went nowhere, set the speed up to six (at least), tell me to push hard for fifty minutes, and then go off to read something. He would come by about every fifteen minutes and check on my progress. If I was doing well, he would ratchet up the speed one (or even two) levels, smile at me, and say, "You can do better."

I would counter with, "I'm sixty-three, you know?"

"That's a young man."

January included an invite in, a trip out, and a trip to Ohio. The first one included Mr. Moon and his wife Susan, Denny McSherry and his wife Pam, and Matt Crost and his wife Mary Lou. They stopped by Lou Malnati's and bought salad and deep-dish pizza. It was a laugh-out-loud night. I was with the three funniest guys I knew, so laughter was at its peak.

I didn't really go out anywhere, so the five-night festival was a big deal. This was all of the musicals put on by Lincolnshire Marriott, and we (Emil and Patty) had four tickets for all of them. Tonight was Mary Poppins, so we looked forward to it. I had a bit of anxiety based on being out for the first time. I had missed the first play, which was in November. We simply sold our seats to someone else.

The first stop was a wholesome hamburger joint, which was near the theatre. I ordered a hamburger, had it cut in half, and struggled with my left hand on the dessert. Emil was driving, and I placed myself in the shotgun seat. We approached the theatre, and Emil dropped us off at the front door. I had to go a long way to the bathroom, and my leg really hurt by the time I went there and back. Plus, I was always watching out for other people. Being in a huge place with lots of people made me nervous.

We made it up in the elevator to the seats in our row. Sitting down was hard, but when I made it, I was ready to enjoy the musical.

And enjoy it I did! The best part I remember was "Feed the Birds." That song made me cry, I think partly in conjunction with my stroke. I was out in public for the first time; I had done it. I was sitting, enjoying the musical with hundreds of people. It was almost if I never had a stroke. It was a grand night.

Finally, it was time to leave, which was supposed to be hard. We were on our feet during the standing ovation, so my legs were ready to go. Emil left to get the car; we had to climb over seats with old people in them (we were the youngest people in the theatre). I took the lead. I slid down to the bottom row, closest to the stage. And then I turned it on. I raced over one row of seats that had no people in them and scampered to the main aisle with seemingly thousands of spectators in it. I never slowed down. I said, "Excuse me," as I fled past surprised elders.

Safe in the elevator, Patty and Joani couldn't stop laughing.

I barreled through the underpass and was waiting patiently for Emil to arrive with the car. Joani grabbed my right leg and thrust me into the car. I was in bed by eleven, two hours past my bedtime. Hopefully, Kyle wouldn't have the treadmill ready for me tomorrow. All I had to do was survive Friday morning.

My daughter Joy was going to celebrate her thirtieth birthday on January 31st. Stephen was planning a surprise birthday bash on Saturday. Joani and I were invited along with her friends from church and Stephen's friends from his Ph.D. program. We debated a long time; Joani felt I shouldn't be out on a long trip. It took about five hours to get to Oxford, Ohio. She had many a sleepless night worrying about whether I would be able to sit still in the car. Finally, we decided we'd go. We brought along Julie, Joy's best friend, to further surprise Joy.

We left on early Saturday morning in the snow. Stephen, Joy, and Charlotte stayed at a spa as his birthday gift to her, while all of their friends decorated the house and cooked the food.

We moved along very slowly. My leg cramped up, and I finally said, "Let's stop at McDonald's."

There was snow that was blowing in the handicapped space, making it hard for me to step down. Plus, my leg was juiced up. I was helped out of the car by Julie and held onto her to walk into the restaurant. The quick movement relieved the pain faster than I thought. I ordered my Coke (nothing tastes like a Coke from McDonald's), and we were back in the car and on our way.

We stopped once more for a lunch break; the snow had ceased. We made it with over an hour to spare. We had met their friends once or twice before, so we knew what to expect. The three of us would hide in the bedroom; then, we would come out. Joy would be surprised, not once, but twice.

It worked. Joy was happy; then, we came out. She burst into tears.

"Mom! Dad!" she said. Then, she saw her best friend. "Ooooh. It's Julie."

She was overjoyed that we had come. The next few hours were devoted to eating all of the deliciously prepared food— including the eleven bags of Donkey Chips we brought—and opening presents. I mostly sat on the couch and basked in the glow, talking to their friends. I had made it to Joy's.

The next day, we all left to go back. One of the bad habits I'd picked up was talking when I shouldn't have talked or gesturing when I shouldn't have gestured. For example, when I wanted Joani to go faster, I'd move my hand quickly forward. I was a back-seat driver from the front seat.

I was made aware of this when we arrived back home. We piled out of the car, and Joani said, "Well, how did you like my driving?"

Julie piped up, "I thought both of you drove marvelously."

Joani looked at me, and there were daggers in her eyes. I cringed. I would have to work on that.

****

Back at RIC, Kyle had questions for me. He was pleased that I made the long trip. He knew he had only two months to force me to improve. His first coup-de-grace was to make me put more weight on my right leg. He accomplished this by making me hold a crutch and tying my left leg up. Then, he made me walk on my crutch and my right leg. He and another girl named (appropriately) Kyle were watching me, when I suddenly started to go backward. I was really scared. I felt like I was going to fall down.

"Kyle!" I screamed. "Help me!"

He only laughed and said, "You aren't going to fall."

I put him down as the meanest man in the world that he would laugh at somebody in dire straits. But, perhaps he felt like I would fall and break my right leg. He never did that "let's tie him up" again. Kyle was getting smart.

Sue was worried about my right arm. She begged me to continue to do the exercises at home to keep it "loose." I kept it "loose" by placing my hand on the kitchen table on top of a towel. Then, I would move it very slowly in each direction until I could open my right hand. It sure impressed Mr. Moon. I also stretched my right arm back and forth until it hit the mark of fifty-five degrees. I could hold it up for a while, and it was so cool.

Sue had it in herself to make me a chef. One day, she dragged me into the kitchen.

"Today, we'll make a peanut butter and jelly sandwich," she said. "You do like pb and j, don't you?"

To tell the truth, it was one of my favorites. "Yes," I said.

"Good. Get everything out."

By this time, I knew where everything was, so I got it out: the peanut butter, the jelly, the bread, the knife, the milk, and the glass. I opened the bread, and I scooped out two pieces. Then came the hard part. It was difficult for me to lift more than a miniscule part of peanut butter out on the bread. Sue let me struggle.

She said, "Why don't you try a spoon?"

A spoon. Huh. I never thought of a spoon.

It made it so much easier. I was able to scoop a large part of peanut butter out of the jar. And I was able to spread it across the bread. I thought, this is easy. Well, easier.

Next came the jelly. The top was skewered on. I turned to Sue. "I can't get it off. Will you do it?"

"You're by yourself. You have to get it off. Here's how." She put the jelly jar under my right arm. "Now, twist."

I twisted. It worked. Sue had taught me a new device.

I used the spoon to scrape the jelly out of the bottom of the jar. It went on easier than the peanut butter. I put the sandwich together. Then, I used my left hand to cut it down the middle.

I used my left hand to pour the milk.

"There. You're done. You can make yourself a sandwich. Don't ever be afraid to try new things."

February and March went by like the winter months they were. I got out more than I should have, because the snowy months were not that snowy at all. In late February, we went to the new Bond movie, *Skyfall*. I got up to the second row; that was all I could make. It was a favorite of my mom, who went with us. I notched another one on my gun belt, another first.

The end of March came by quickly. I was counting the days until I was released from my prison. The last day I met with Kristina, and she had prepared a giant book the likes of which

I had never seen before. It was all the exercises we had worked on over the past four months. I was thankful to her for all the work she put into this. If I'd only known how persistent Joani was going to be at making me do this.

Kyle spent the last few days making up some exercises for me to do on my own. The last time we were together (or so I thought), he let me play WII "bowling." I was a good bowler, but not as good as Kyle. I had to bowl with my left hand, and Kyle bowled a turkey, in other words, three strikes in a row.

The day before Good Friday finally came. I would miss Kristina, Sue, and even Kyle. I bowed out at 3:00, and all the people I would miss came out to hug me and say good-bye.

I said, "I will miss all of you. All you have to do is try your best. These people are here to make you better."

Kyle walked over to me and gave me the biggest hug he could give someone.

He said, "I will miss teasing you. You're the best person I've ever teased."

So that's what it was. Here, I thought, he was mean.

CHAPTER 9

I was back at John Hersey High School. I had cleaned every-thing out except the closet and the file cabinets. It was the end of my seventeenth year, and for some reason I was being transferred to Prospect High School. I still had to finish my classes for the week, giving the final exams for the semester. I was morose as could be, and I couldn't figure out why they were doing this to me. I had been a good teacher.

At the end of the day, I opened up my closet; it was full. I started to empty the closet, swearing I would be the best teacher I could be at Prospect. I stopped down at the English office and was amazed I didn't clean out my mailbox for over six months. Well, I started to go through it. There were notices for field trips I had missed; there were notices to call parents in there, some as far back as three months ago.

I still had to drive to Prospect to see what my schedule looked like for the following August. I made the trek (it wasn't too far), and I met with the English division head. She had screwed me. She said the only classes she had for me were kids who hated school and didn't want to be there. She said she was sorry. Oh, by the way, I'd have to move around to five rooms; I'd have no room of my own. She said the good thing about these classes were that they'd be small in number; some students would even drop out.

I slumped into the driver's seat of my car and gunned away. I was scalding mad. I thrashed my fist, and suddenly woke up. So, that was it—a dream, rather a nightmare. The weird thing about it was I didn't remember any other dream before that. I was going to be haunted with nightmares about my old school building almost every night. Sometimes classes, sometimes the end in sight. There was one thing I got back—my ability to

49

dream—something that had been missing from me for seven months.

I could also turn over to the left side, and dangle my arm over my chest. I was almost sleeping on my stomach.

My wife had to come up with things for me to do. It was now April, so I could walk outside. She started walking with me down to the end of the block, (which was really uphill), turn around, and walk back down. It was one house at a time—hellish in nature. I crawled alongside her as best as I could. With each step, I felt like I was going to fall down. I leaned to the left so much that I often landed with my left foot on the grass. I also had to keep my eyes down, so I wouldn't slip on some errant twig or some crack on the sidewalk.

She was always helpful, saying things like, "Good job! You can do it!"

I was dog-tired. I laugh now when I look back and see what little I did.

Joani took me out to Costco and Barnes and Noble. She took it upon herself to make sure I did as much walking as I could.

One day in early May, I made the decision to walk a quarter of a mile. Joani was with me. My IT band was hurting on the left side as much as I could stand it. So, I stood still about half the time. What an ecstasy I felt when I finished! Needless to say, I collapsed into my Lazy-Boy chair and downed a full glass of water (with ice).

One night, I went walking with Mr. Moon. This was later on when I could make the quarter-mile without stopping at all. So, I was proud to be able to do it with Mr. Moon. We made our way around the block, with me talking as little as possible.

When we were finished, Mr. Moon said, "I didn't know you took so long and had so much trouble wheezing."

"Now you know," I said, breathlessly. "It takes a whole lot out of me. And that's only a quarter-mile."

I finally went a half-mile. That was with Joani. It started out just as difficult as the previous quarter-mile. But, after one or two stops, I made it. And, from that point on, I made the half-mile my scenic route, once taking it without Joani. I was learning to walk!

50

That spring, we had to make a decision about who was going to cut the grass and trim the bushes. Joani talked to a friend and decided on Tino. For two years, he's patiently cut the grass every Friday, and boy, does he trim.

In late May, we had to go see Dr. Marinko. I was really looking forward to visiting him. He had talked me into feeling good about myself and said that in time, I would heal. I couldn't wait to tell him my wheelchair was gone (in the basement), I walked a half-mile without so much as a crutch, and I talked reasonably well. My right arm didn't move, but one thing at a time.

I was delighted to see him, smiling as usual. What he surprised me with was the two novels (*Ten Again* and *First Time Around*) that I had given him when I left Alexian Brothers. I had not autographed them, because my left arm didn't write well enough. Now, it did (slowly). I took time to sign each novel for him. (He hadn't read them yet. It was not time for me to find out that he didn't have motivation to read, maybe with all the doctor's work he had to do.)

He was happy to see me as well. He talked for a while, made me promise that I was going to do things, other than the exercises, with my right arm. He had me walk to see what I did, and seemed all right with it.

Then, he smiled and said, "Well, this piece of paper should give you two more months at therapy. Work hard!"

Joani jumped for joy. I was downcast; I wasn't through with Kyle yet.

We went around visiting the therapists, who were ecstatic to see me. One man said, "Look at him walking!"

All were thrilled to see me again.

In early June, I had Joani give me my bath, dressed myself to kill, and prepared for therapy at RIC in Wheeling. Kyle was there. Thankfully, it was only three times a week (Monday, Wednesday, Friday), and half-days only. At least they wouldn't slay me, and I'd have the summer months off.

They all had big plans. Let's start with Kyle.

"Well, you came back. Let's see if we can work you into shape."

Actually, he was glad that I walked a half-mile every day; he chose to make it a mile before the summer was out. He knew I wasn't scared of the treadmill anymore, so he planned to get me on the device at least two times a week, and the sit-down bike once a week. He knew I liked the six-minute trial, so he would push me to do better, breaking my record every time. He tried old machinery once or twice, a battery-packed device that would make my right leg twitch up whenever I lifted it, causing my leg to get stronger. That didn't work very well. And, since it was nice outside, he took me for long walks, letting me rest whenever I felt I needed to. In truth, he was working me up to a mile.

The six-minute trial was taking off. Every time, I passed the previous time limit. Nothing made me feel as good. I was getting faster and better.

One day, he worked me hard, walking laps around the gym. Then, with only six minutes left, he said, "Let's do the time trial."

"What?" I stated. "There's not enough time left to do that."

"There's enough time, if you move it. C'mon, let's go!"

I was exhausted and angry. But, this meant so much to me, I hunkered down and gave it my best go. I felt that I even went faster the last two or three laps. I did it! I knew I had beaten my record!

"Well, what was the time?" I said, barely breathing.

He told me.

"You're kiddin'. Let me see that."

He showed me. "It doesn't matter."

I was so mad I didn't speak to Kyle for the rest of the day. Joani could tell when she picked me up. It was the only day I could truly say I was mad. Kyle could say he was trying to help me, and then he sets up a rotten thing like that.

Joani talked to me and calmed me down. She said it serves me right if I was mad, but that she expected me to apologize to Kyle and be done with it. I could see she was right. Kyle, like everyone else there, had my best interests at heart, and if I was too foolish to see it, well, I could just not work and not get better.

"I'm sorry, Kyle. I didn't mean to get all fired up like that."

"That's all right. I expect people to get mad once in a while. Listen up. I've got a surprise for you. We're going to go play miniature golf on Friday."

"What? Really? Can I golf? I mean, with one hand."

"You can't golf, you know, you never could." Kyle smiled. "We're going to take a bunch of people along. You'll be fine. Trust me."

On Friday, Kyle yelled, "Okay. Go to the bathroom if you have to, and then meet at the front door. We're going to go golfing."

Sue was coming along. She was going to be my chaperone. Kyle drove the van, and divvyed the people up, with him taking the "challenging" ones.

We had a good group of three, with Sue watching, not playing. We all played our hearts out, understanding the game, and we all scored fairly well. I hit the ball with my left hand, and I hit it straight, once even scoring a hole in one. Sue grabbed me to help me navigate a hill, but otherwise, I did all right. It was a pleasure to play, and it was sure better than doing those exercises.

Sue had good ideas for me now that it was nice outside. She made sure we always did the stretches, had me cook like crazy, but asked me how I was doing in the garden.

"We have a gardener. He cuts the grass, trims the bushes, and even pulls the weeds." (This last piece of information I knew was NOT true.)

Sue gave me a surprised look. "You're sure your wife doesn't do some of the weeding?"

"Well," I admitted, "maybe some."

She had me. "It's pleasant out. I'll gather the tools."

Sue picked out some tools, a plastic bag, and a chair for me to sit on. There was a hedge that was littered with several weeds and scraps of paper. I cursed the people who threw away pieces of paper; the weeds were meant to grow. I bent over to pull the weeds out, reaching ever so slightly, so I wouldn't fall off the chair.

At my convenience, I slid off the chair. I was now crippled on one side, a feeling that I didn't take as too comforting. I tried, but couldn't do anything that I was meant to do, including slide down to my next position.

Sue said, "You're too heavy to lift you up. I'll go get Kyle."

Oh, great. First, she tells me I'm too fat to lift up. Then, she goes and gets Kyle, who will only make fun of me some more.

While I was resting there, a man who I didn't know came up to me. He said, "Can I help you up, mister? You look rather helpless."

Suddenly, Kyle appeared. "That's all right. I can help him up."

Without so much as a "cut" in my direction, Kyle helped me up with Sue holding the chair.

"Thanks, Kyle."

"You're welcome," said Kyle. "We should have left poor Mike out here in the sun to see when he would've called for help."

Sue asked me to stand up, which I could do, and move my chair to the next position. I proceeded to pull the weeds out and pick up the paper until the row of bushes looked nice.

"There," Sue said. "You can do it. We'll have to ask your wife to set out a chair for you, and you can be every bit a help on weeds as the next man."

I was most pleased with Kristina, who saw a big improvement in my speech. It was totally frustrating to forget words from time to time, though.

"Look," said Kristina, "you're not any less intelligent than you once were. You just forget words from brain to mouth. I cannot imagine what you're going through right now. But, if you keep working, you'll get better. Just talk when you can talk. And don't stop talking—whatever you do."

It was hard to see her words as hopeful. I mean, I couldn't say words like I used to. And I forgot so many words from time to time. Sometimes I could say words easily, and sometimes not at all. As more social situations arose, I would find time to use them once again. Don't give up, I told myself. And don't forget—talk slowly.

Finally, I forced myself, when Joani was not with me, to go the extra mile. The mile nearly wore me out. I rested a couple of times, and finally made it home—in a half hour. I collapsed into the Lazy-Boy chair and rested for a full hour.

But I was up and rested when Joani came home. "Guess what?" I said. "I walked a mile."

She was ecstatic, and so was Kyle. "So, you made it. About time."

Oh, you couldn't keep old Kyle down.

One day, I met another man. And he wasn't just another man. He was Mark Kirk, a patient who had had a major stroke and a United States Senator. He made great strides, and I was happy to call him a friend. He surprised us his last day by giving us gifts, the U.S. Senate Seal with a note and his autograph.

****

It was July. I wanted to make some more headway on my stroke, so I thought it was about time I moved out of the kids' bathroom, where I received a bath from Joani, to my bathroom where I could shower myself. Joani moved the bench in, so I could sit down and give myself a bath.

That worked not at all. I almost slipped and fell getting out of the bench. So, the next day Joani removed the bench, and I could stand up and, for the first time since the stroke, give myself a shower. I've never gone back.

Suddenly, my graduation was here.

Kyle said I was with him for the last hour, so I could do anything I wanted to. I had bowled with him a few times, and I wanted to beat him.

"You die!" I said.

"It's your funeral," Kyle responded.

I had him after the first frame. I had a spare; he had only a nine. He grimaced.

55

I had only my left leg to balance on, and my left arm to throw the ball via the WII game. But, I was a bowling champion. Ha! Ha!

His next six scores were strikes—a double turkey. Game over.

My graduation was hopeful. I could do certain things I couldn't do before. It was August 9th. I was almost one year into my stroke. The next year would prove wonderful.

CHAPTER 10

I approached Rick Wager, and told him that August 17th was almost here. He promised to have both Joani and me up in front of the church to tell the members what last year had been like. I was sure what I was going to say, but not sure if I could get the words out.

As we sat there and listened to the opening hymns, I was nervous. Rick called us up and spoke first.

"God confuses me from time to time. I don't know why he chose to have Mike suffer a stroke. But he did. And Mike has shown reliance on Jesus, and not getting down on himself at all. He has made a remarkable comeback, and he's even agreed to come back as a permanent greeter. I'd like to turn the mic over to Joani first and then Mike."

Joani spoke first about how the church was instrumental in helping her cope with the seriousness of the situation. Then, Joani turned the microphone over to me.

I started to stumble, but Rick helped me immensely when he said these words: "Take your time."

I relaxed, and everything came to me. "I'd like to start by saying I'm deeply thankful to everyone in this church. Joani and I came to this church seven years ago. We came to the Thanksgiving feast, where Dan and Leslie made three soups— yeah, that many." (There was laughter. I was churning now.) "We didn't know anybody, except maybe a few. Now, we know everybody. If only I could remember their names. I'd like to publicly thank everyone here for showing what Christian love is to us. I'd like to thank you for all the great cards, for the welcome back to church, and especially for helping Joani when she needed it most. God bless you!"

I had done it! Rick (or Jesus) helped me get through this with little or no slip-ups. I sat down with relief, and the spirit of one year came and went. A man that I had never seen bolted over to see me after the church service. He claimed to have an artificial leg brace that would help me walk more evenly and with greater confidence. I tried it on, and immediately I felt better. He told me I could have it—for free. I wore it some days, and some days I didn't. Boy, did God have a say in that one?

My next task was greeting. I felt it was important letting the members see me standing and welcoming them to church every Sunday. This way, they would hopefully be put in the right mood. I would be a "stealth" greeter, one who goes back and forth to each door. That way, I would see every person. I received hugs from everybody, telling me to "walk forward and not fail." My biggest problem was going back and forth and not falling. However, I didn't fall, and thereby gained confidence every day.

Over the summer, I helped out with the "Food Bank." This was a gargantuan effort that made the community feel special. It brought out more than one hundred people.

My first task was to help Jesse (the youngest girl of Dan and Leslie) make bags of popcorn. This was for adults and children. The adults would get numbers based on when they got there. Then, there wouldn't be any cheating in line. (There was enough food for everybody; we just didn't want chaos to ensue.)

Next, Joani would call the number, and five would go through the line. There was a caregiver for everybody, helping them to load up with food and escort them to their car. It was always a pleasant day. One time, it threatened rain, but it never happened.

Meanwhile, I sat behind the big table with two other girls. I gave out snacks—grapes, grape juice, cookies, and water. I was tempted to eat cookies, but I limited myself to seven.

****

When I was at RIC Wheeling, the therapists told me I could drive. Say what? Sue even set aside several sessions to practice the left-footed drive machine, and I took the symbols test to see if I could remember it. Everyone was up for it, except me. I made my way, with Joani, to the Alexian Brothers Rehabilitation Hospital for a 1:00 appointment.

The first person I saw was a lady who tested my eyes and my right leg to make sure I was strong enough. I told her I didn't think I was that strong. She confirmed that. Then, she gave me the symbols test, which I had scored 100% at RIC. How about 60%? I never saw such messed-up symbols in my life. I had only been off the road for a year, not nine years. She marked it, and she told me she'd see how I did on the highway.

The next person was Dennis. He escorted me to a small car, which he said we would be in for two hours. It was fixed for left-handed driving with a bar sticking out of the steering wheel. He also had put on it a left-footed drive machine, which allowed me to use only my left foot to drive. My right foot was perched over the accelerator, which had a cap on it, and was therefore unable to drive. The brake was in the same place, and the accelerator was to the left. The hard part was going to be using the left foot to drive. I was used to using the right foot to drive.

"All right," he said, "now get comfortable."

How hard was this going to be? I hadn't driven in a year, and I was supposed to drive with my left foot.

"Now, start the engine."

Here was another problem. I had to reach my left hand across the steering wheel, put the key in, and turn it.

"Here's how you do it." He showed me a trick about positioning the wheel, so I could get my hand in easily. "Whenever you're ready, blast ahead."

I had to reach my left hand across my body and grab the gearshift. I did it and put it in drive. At least I didn't have to back out. I was ready. I took a deep breath and lifted my foot off the brake. I punched the gas and watched it go. And go it went. I moved my foot quickly back to the brake, and we jammed to a stop. Oh, yeah, I was ready to drive again. One thing I was impressed with was how fast he was. I mean, he had to be. He had a driver's instructor brake on his side. At least I couldn't smash the car up.

We finally made it out of the parking lot. I made sure I stopped behind the stop sign, and Dennis said, "Turn left."

My hardest problem was turning left. I punched too hard, and the car swerved left and then right. "Oh, brother, I'm sorry."

"That's okay. Just relax. We'll stay back here for a while until you get the feel of it."

Back here was mid-suburbia. Every bit of dark black pavement was waiting for me. And there wasn't a car in sight. Dennis had planned it well. His two-hours-long drive fit in very well. Back here were plenty of stop signs, so I could get the feel of the car. There were plenty of pavements, so I could learn to pull over to the side and then start again. There were plenty of school parking lots (without students), so I could practice parking. Dennis figured out there was time in between my looking over my shoulder to see what madman was coming too fast from my rear. So, he talked. He mostly talked about the road rules.

"My rule has always been 'Look out for bikes. They are the fastest guys on the road.' or 'Do you see any kids down there? They come super fast.' or 'Do you see any cars backing up?'" It was hard to concentrate.

I wanted him to know that I was always the safest guy on the highway. "You know, I've been driving since 1966, and I've never been involved in an accident. Not when I was driving."

"That's good. Now, turn right."

We were back at the parking lot. "Finally," I breathed aloud.

"No, we're going to drive up to the forest."

I noticed we were in loads of traffic. We were at a red light. I waited for it to turn green, and then I went ahead.

"Turn left up here."

Dennis took me into the forest, where there weren't many cars. He had me pull into a parking lot, and then had me practice parking going backward.

After one back in, I put the car in park.

"Really good." said Dennis. "And you missed the trash can."

I didn't even see the trash can.

After that, we went back to the parking lot, I put it in park, and turned off the engine. I breathed a sigh of relief.

"Well, let's go in. That's enough for your first day."

My first day? I thought he would pass me after this. If I'd thought about it, we didn't go out onto any major highways, plus he didn't take me out on the freeway. A must.

Dennis said, "We'll see you back next week at this time."

Next week, I was back at 1:00. I bitched to my wife that I had driven enough to have my license renewed. She disagreed. She felt it was better that I had as much time behind the wheel with a trained veteran with a brake on his side. Joani tended to pray the entire time I was gone.

Dennis upped it all around Elk Grove. He started me back in the neighborhood where I could get the feel of the car. Then, he slowly moved me onto the busy highways with the motorists who just didn't care. I didn't relax for a very long time. We pulled into parking lots, where he made me do all kinds of parking.

One time, I was third in line behind a fellow who was going to turn left when the green arrow came on. Dennis always said, "Leave about three spaces between you and the person in front of you."

That seemed rather excessive to me, but I obeyed. Suddenly, the green arrow came on. He started, and then stopped. I was quick. I slammed on the brake, just in time to avoid causing an accident. I looked at him and said, "Sorry."

At the end of the afternoon, just when I thought I was going to go back to the parking lot, he steered me past the lot to the Elk Grove Library. He had me do a parking trick or two, and then he had me go out. We stopped at the stop sign, and I forgot to put my blinker on.

"You forgot to put your blinker on," Dennis said.

There was nobody around. I said, "Sorry."

When we got back, he said, "Now, what did you do wrong?"

"Well," I said, "I obviously forgot to put my blinker on. And, oh, yeah, I had to stop fast when that bonehead started and then stopped so suddenly."

Dennis smiled. He said, "I put on my brake so you wouldn't hit him."

"What?" I didn't believe him because I didn't see him. Like I said before he was fast.

"Yeah, I did it, all right," Dennis reiterated.

So, that was it. I had to make it through two hours without him catching any mistake.

Next week, I was back at 1:00.

He took me out to Elmhurst from Elk Grove. Those who don't know the route will be surprised that this is fairly long. I'll give him credit; he knew his route. We went up and down and around every hill there was. We went on roads that I didn't know about, and I had grown up in the Chicago area. I remember the scariest part of the journey was the time he had me go into this church. It was built on a hill. And what a hill! He had me stop at the top of it, and then back up. I wanted to tell him I wouldn't be doing anything he had planned (like kill us), but I didn't think he wanted to hear it.

We parked all around Elmhurst. Then he asked me to parallel park. I meant to say I've never parked this way since my driver's test. But, I kept my mouth shut and tried to do it. On the fourth try, I barely got it.

I was roaring mad when he didn't pass me again. I would have to come back two more times, for a grand total of ten hours.

On the last time, Dennis did what I knew he was going to finally do. He took me out on the freeway.

He said, "Now, watch your speed. And don't come up beside a car. He may move from side to side and crash into you."

In other words, don't pass anyone.

I took the expressway rather calmly, and I knew I was good to go. When he took me back to the parking lot, he said, "Well, I think I can pass you."

I smiled at Joani.

Dennis said, "I had to get used to you. To make sure you could handle the machine. You did well. Now, take your time and don't go out in the car more than one hour. And have someone along with you. You'll be fine."

I shook his hand. We were done. I had passed one more milestone. I had the freedom to drive.

CHAPTER 11

Some time in early September, I received an invitation that was a year overdue. My good friend, Anne Singleton, asked me to share with her students a book that they'd been reading, *Ten Again.* I was supposed to talk about my book after leading a discussion on revision, the true art of writing. I was to share first with Jen Weiss, a lady who taught my book for summer reading. Then, I would move to Anne's class. If there was any problem with the setup, it was that all three classes were first, second, and fourth period. It would mean I'd have to get up very early, shower and dress, and fight the rush hour traffic to arrive on time to Libertyville High School, which was a good forty minutes away. Other than that, I would have to talk clearly, a skill that I had not mastered.

When I received the email, I hesitated a long while. It was just over a year since I'd had my stroke, and I wasn't confident at all that I could talk. I finally decided to do it because Anne was my friend, and I'd let her down last year. So, I sent her a return telling her to name her date and I'd be there. It was the scariest email I'd ever written.

I didn't sleep much the night before, and I woke up in plenty of time. One thing that I had going for me was that the first two hours would go by in a dream; I wouldn't wake up until fourth period.

I dressed neatly, ate a small breakfast, and climbed in the car. Joani was driving. The main reason I had her along was to fill in the words for me when I forgot what came next. I sat motionless, and thought about what I would say. More than anything, I wanted to get out.

We made it in record time. There was obviously no snow, so we didn't have to suddenly narrow-down to one lane. I had forgotten what a high school looked like until we got out; it had been over a year since I'd been to one. Shorts and t-shirts were the clothes de jour, and sleepiness was on everyone's mind. This will be easy, I thought, they'd sleep through it all.

We signed in with the hall guard, although he misspelled my last name. Then, we met Anne. She was delighted to see us.

"Hi. You made it okay," she smiled.

She took us up in the elevator. Needless to say, it was the slowest elevator in the world. Then, we met Jen. Before I knew it, her class was starting to file in. The bell finally rang. It was "go" time.

I started with the one thing I think I could say: "I've had a stroke. As you can see, I'm standing on both feet behind the podium (it was there just to catch me if I fell), my right arm doesn't go up, and it's hard to talk. I didn't know, a year ago when I had the stroke, that a person would lose their ability to talk—I mean completely—so this is how I talk, get used to it. So, any questions?"

I was their teacher and they were my students, just like the old days. I had started with what seemed an easy statement, and I'd made it this far through. I'd mastered something I'd taken forty years to achieve, and it felt like Heaven.

"I've got a question. How did you learn to talk?"

Oh, boy, she thinks I can talk. "Well, I started out by knowing one word, 'no.' Then, I learned by reading and talking as much as I could. My therapist taught me, 'You're as smart as ever. Don't let anyone tell you you're not as intelligent. It's hard when you can visualize the word, but it won't come to you.' I'm sure I'll be more verbose in a year from now."

"Any other questions?" I asked.

They seemed satisfied. I turned to Joani. "This is my wife, Joani, with whom I could not have gotten along. She will pass out some of my rough draft and some of my hard copy, and I'll show you how revision works."

When the first two pages of both were passed out, I began my lecture. "As you can see, I always begin my rough draft by handwriting it. I was an English teacher, and so I always

Michael J. Bellito

had plenty of papers to grade. The outline for this story was done in July, 2002. I started writing in 2006, the first time I had motivation to write. I wrote this from May to December, and then I typed from January to May. One year to surprise my mom, who didn't know I was writing a novel. But, the key to writing it this way was I'd always have time for revision. Turn now to page one of my rough draft, and I'll show you how I'd revise."

This was going better than I'd thought. Next, I showed them how I'd changed the title for Chapter 8. Then, I worked my way through the page, pointing out all the cross-outs and re-writes.

"Who can tell me why I wrote this line, 'came crashing down like a Soviet missile from the sky'?"

Nobody moved. I've got them. They weren't alive during this time, so they have no idea what a Soviet missile was used for—or they didn't pay attention in history class.

One brave girl spoke up, "It was because of the Cold War."

"Right!" I shouted. "Well, that's it on revision. Anybody have any questions about the novel?"

The teacher had written down their questions the day before, so she asked most of them. More students asked their own questions the next two periods; it was because they were sleepy the first period, and even I, with all my wit and banter, couldn't appeal to them.

"Is most of this true?"

"Yes, most of it is true. Look, I fantasized some of it to make it seem funny. My kids would come up to me and asked me if this really happen. I'd say, 'Yes, but it was written in such a way to make it humorous.' Thus, revision always worked its way into the script." Oh, I was on now.

"Let me give you an example. I met Walt Disney. But, it was really five years later, four months before he died. And my Dad took a picture of him. All that is true. But, it couldn't have fit into the story unless it happened then, when I was eleven, instead of sixteen. Now, that's not particularly humorous, but it's just an example of where I changed things."

"How did he dic?" asked a student who was now suddenly awake.

I stated, "He went into the hospital on November 2nd because he didn't feel well. And the doctor told him he had cancer and would have to have one lung removed. Do you know how many cigarettes he smoked?"

Nobody knew.

"Two and a half packs a day. The animators always knew he was coming because they would hear his cough down the hall. He firmly believed cigarettes did not cause cancer. We know better now. Well, he had the lung removed November 7th, and then the doctor told him the bad news. He had, at most, only two years to live. It took only six weeks. Walt Disney died on December 15th, 1966, ten days after his sixty-fifth birthday. His nine old animators lived long past him. And his wife lived until 1997, thirty-one years after he died. She had a stroke on December 15th, and died the next day."

The class was now spellbound.

"Disney had an apartment built above the fire station in Disneyland, and for the last eleven years of his life, he spent almost every weekend there, watching the little kids flowing into the park. His wife kept that apartment close to her for the next thirty-one years."

The class applauded and then filed out. I had done it. I had only asked my wife for help when I didn't know what word to say about five times. I couldn't move my right leg, but that was all right. I could still hold a class in awe, I told myself.

The next two periods went by even more smoothly. During third period, when I took a much-deserved rest, Paul Reiff, the school's English Department Chair, came up to visit me in Anne's class. He brought me a Libertyville blanket to keep me warm during the winter.

Anne gave me the essays she had the students write covering *Ten Again*. This was a surprise because I didn't know they wrote about my book. They could write about the characters, the word choice, or the plot. I didn't have to grade them; I only read them for fun.

All in all, the day was a huge success. We rode home, and all I could talk about was how kind the students were to me and how they treated me with such respect. I had made it. I was a teacher again.

After I got home, I slept for two hours, or maybe three.

****

Later that month, I made another lecture on *Ten Again;* this time the students were reading it as part of their curriculum. It was at Rolling Meadows High School, and it was part of Susan's Popular Literature class. I was surprised when I received her email because I wasn't expecting it. It read: "Hi, I'm Susan, and I'm teaching your *Ten Again* novel as part of my curriculum. Would you be willing to come in and talk to the students about what they have read?"

I emailed her right back and said, "I'd be pleased to tell any stories you might like to hear." I felt this was a second chance to be what I was made to be, a teacher.

I arrived, with Joani, one bright afternoon. There would be no revision; there was no writing about this. I would stand up there and wax on about anything I felt like, provided they asked good questions.

I started out meeting with Susan, and more of a delight she could not have been. I gave her a copy of *First Time Around,* and told her this was a better story than *Ten Again.* I told her my third novel *Abner's Story* was coming out later this year, and if she liked the Cubs, she was sure to like this one. She said her class was anxious to meet me, and she told them I was recovering from a stroke. Finally, the one and only class arrived.

I began the way I had begun with the Libertyville classes, telling them how I had my stroke, and telling them what I felt like. I told them the worst part, by far, was how I had lost my ability to talk, not the best thing for a speech teacher.

Then, I told them about my two books and how *First Time Around* dealt with teenage angst and bullying. I also told them that *Ten Again* dealt with (mostly) true stories while my second book was real fiction; only bits and pieces were things that actually happened to me. I said I was proudest of *First Time Around* because it was the true work of an artist, creating fiction.

They listened politely, and then they were free to ask questions. "Is there any part of *Ten Again* that's not true?"

"Almost all of it's true; I know, I lived it." I hesitated a minute. "Well, you don't remember the 'Bozo Show,' do you?"

They shook their heads in unison.

"I was never on the 'Bozo Show.' My son Matt was. I asked him if I could borrow this episode, and he said, 'Sure.' Do any of you know how popular Bozo was?"

Once again, they shook their heads, a decided 'no.'

"Bozo was more popular than the Bears or the Blackhawks were. They stopped selling tickets to fans after ten years. That's right, I said ten years."

Astonished, the class looked at each other.

"One of my good friends, Diane, was pregnant with her second child. She bought tickets, so he (it turned out to be a boy) could one day see Bozo live. He did, when he was in the third grade. They bought six tickets, so their older daughter could go along with a friend, and Chad invited Matt, who was seven years old. The other two fathers—not me—were going to take them."

The class was all ears now. I knew how to hook a bunch of students.

"Three or four weeks before the show, I'd come home from work and saw Matt practicing with a Ping-Pong ball and six buckets. He'd always say, 'This is so I'll do well when I get picked by the Bozo-Puter to play the Grand Prize Game.'"

I sat him down. "Matt, I don't want you to feel disappointed when you don't get chosen. There are a lot of boys there."

He was adamant.

"Finally, the day came. It was on a Monday—taped—so everybody who wanted to see the show could do so the next Monday. I went off to work, and promptly forgot about the show for the duration. Finally, eighth hour came around, and I had off. A colleague of mine answered the phone, and said, 'Mike, it's for you. It's Matt.'"

"I thought to myself, 'Why's Matt calling me? He should be in school.'"

"I picked up the phone. Matt said, 'Hey, Dad, guess what?' (Then, it all came to pass.) I said, 'What did you get?' He answered, 'Five.'"

The students applauded.

"And that was the true story. Obviously, the kid in *Ten Again* had to do considerably worse. I taped it, and Matt shows his classes—he's in his thirteenth year at Vernon Hills High School—every year. Also, the relatives who lived in Iowa and as far away as California saw it on television the next week."

The day had gone by fast. And one thing I knew I could say, it felt good to be a teacher again.

CHAPTER 12

It was time to go to Ohio once more. It was little Charlotte's first birthday, September 24th. I had been driving for a week now; I even went over to RIC, with Joani, to show everybody what I had accomplished. So, it was without hesitation that I asked Joani if I could drive at least part of the way to Ohio.

"What? Are you crazy?"

"Well, why not? If I don't drive, I'm never gonna get any better."

"Look at it from my point of view. If we have an accident, then we're not going to be there for Charlotte's birthday."

I scrunched up my face.

"Look, I can drive. I've done it before. Please just let me do it. You let me drive to RIC, remember?" I asked.

"I've had nightmares about it since."

So, that was that. I had to learn that Joani did not feel comfortable with me behind the steering wheel. I could drive with anyone else—just not her.

The trip to Ohio was without incident. Probably if I'd driven, we'd have run off the road or run over sixteen people. We both were happy that I could now make the trip without having to stop often. I was fine, especially at McDonald's.

We arrived at Joy's school around three in the afternoon. She was no longer a first-grade teacher; she was a literacy coach. We met her in her office. She was overjoyed to see us. Tomorrow would be a big day for Charlotte; it would be a Hungry Caterpillar day.

We spent the night with Stephen, eating dinner and getting to know Charlotte. I would tease her by looking around the condiments on the table and moving my good hand to "visit"

71

her. She laughed. It was as if she knew the celebration for her first birthday was tomorrow.

Joy outdid herself. (What did I expect? She was Joy, after all.) After Charlotte went down for her two- to three-hour nap; we got to work.

There was a picture for every month of her life on the wall. There was every kind of food you could imagine—Stephen's friends were bringing all their recipes. There were balloons hanging down from the ceiling. And there were Hungry Caterpillars everywhere. I mean everywhere. They were on the walls, the tables, and the chairs.

Stephen's friends started arriving just as Charlotte was waking up. She was amazed at all the people who had come to visit her. She sat on the floor and opened presents—one toy after another.

Joy finally set Charlotte down in her high chair with nothing on except her diaper. This giant chocolate cake with red and white frosting was set down in front of her. Luke and Ryan were very picky eaters. Charlotte ate everything, and she looked at the twins like they were nuts to be leaving this much good food on their plates. So, she munched on the cake, getting half of it on her forehead, her cheeks, her chin, and her body. We all laughed; she didn't mind. She just chuckled as she scarfed down the cake.

This reminded me of Luke's and Ryan's first birthday, when they each got their own cake to eat. Luke did okay, but Ryan got a massive amount of cake in his eye and started to cry. He slept in Grammy's arms while Luke opened all the presents. Some birthday!

We went to church the next day, and then we headed home. Joani drove all the way.

****

I was walking every day, and getting faster all the time. I sometimes walked a mile, but more often a half-mile. Mr. Moon invited me to homecoming at John Hersey High School. This would be a real test. I pictured: myself standing tall and greeting people for three hours. Could I last that long?

Mr. Moon picked me up at seven. The night was chill, but not too cold. We decided to wear our matching outfits—Olympic jackets. These weren't just any jackets, either. They were red, white, and blue, and on the back of the jacket was an eagle swooping down on the five colors of the Olympic rings. What a sight!

We piled out of the car, and it was Heaven-sent. I stood and moved and wasn't afraid as tons of Hersey people came out of the woodwork to salute me. There were lots of people from the olden days too, most of whom I didn't recognize. In the south end zone, there was the Class of '83, celebrating their thirtieth reunion, plus the Class of '03, back ten years. They were glad to see me, although most of them didn't know I'd had a stroke.

I was most happy to see my friends, who were still teaching at Hersey. I had been out eight years already, but it seemed like I'd never left. A big surprise, and one I'd never expected to see, was Amy Jabocson, a graduate from the Class of '87. She was ecstatic to see me, and we were reminded of when she came into my Mass Media class to tell about her adventures as a broadcast journalist when she first started out.

I had finally talked to every person I could think of, without moving more than five yards. It was a solid three hours; I had made it. We slowly moved back to the car, which was parked not very far away. I had Mr. Moon help me into the car; I was too weak to do it myself. I collapsed inside the shotgun seat. I was exhausted. "Let's go home."

"Not yet. There's one more must-stop before we go home. You remember what it is, don't you?"

I thought about it for several minutes; then it hit me.

DQ—I had only had a Dairy Queen once since my stroke. My mind was weak, but my stomach was strong. I said, "Okay. As long as I don't have to get out and purchase my own ice cream. You know what I want—Mint Oreo Blizzard."

Then Mr. Moon did something he'd never done before. He said, "One Mint Oreo Blizzard, coming up. It's my treat."

It tasted better than any Blizzard I'd ever had.

****

Trunk-or-Treat. No, I didn't spell it wrong. It was trunk, as in car, where the candy would be hidden. First, they had to play a game of some sort, made up by the owner of the automobile. The night was held at church on the Monday before Halloween, with Awana—"Approved Workmen Are Not Ashamed." That way the hosts would be sure they had enough students there, and the kids could try out their costumes. It turned out to be the coldest night of the year so far. We had no trouble filling the parking lot, and there was a fire down at one end to keep the children warm.

The parents all dressed up. I was a farmer—no, I did not use my gorilla-man costume. And Joani was a lady with lots of pockets, which held treats. I was made to sit by the candy. And Joani would run the game. As I recall, it involved the kids chucking something round, and they had to "win" a piece of candy by placing it over a bowling pin. Joani was a real stickler with the candy.

We asked Matt to bring his twins, Luke and Ryan. Joy surprised us by visiting with Charlotte. So, everybody would be together. Charlotte was as cute as she could be, a ladybug costume. Luke and Ryan were identical bats.

They visited us about halfway through. Luke and Ryan thought Charlotte was cuter than peach pie, and wanted to kiss her over and over. Charlotte knew why she was there; she wanted candy. She started to say, "Candy. Candy. Candy."

Joy was meeting with old friends for picture taking. I was getting stiff-legged by sitting around all night, and, as the cold bothered my leg more than anything, I felt I had to get up. I got up and made my way toward the sanctuary, to warm up as much as anything. I used the bathroom while I was there, and was surprised to see the twins sitting around when I came out. Well, maybe they had to warm up.

I sat down, and we looked through their candy.

"Wow! This is a lot of candy. It's lucky you guys came tonight."

"That's nothing," said Luke. "Halloween comes sometime later this week, and we're going to pack it in."

I laughed. "Halloween is Thursday, and you're really going to 'pack it in.' In spite of the rain."

They looked up in fear. Ryan said, "Rain? What rain?"

"It's supposed to warm up and rain on Halloween. But, if you don't like the weather in Chicago, wait five minutes, it'll change. Don't worry, boys, it'll be fine."

They breathed a sigh of relief. I was wrong of course; it rained like the dickens. Joani and I made the trek out to Matt's house. It took over an hour because of the rain.

"Well, what're you going to do?" I asked.

"We're going out," Matt answered.

By the time Matt and Becki got Luke and Ryan ready, it had stopped raining. It was actually warm outside. So, Joani and I manned the candy and gave it out to anyone who came. Joani gushed at anybody who looked "awesome."

They were gone about an hour. They went around the long block, and didn't come back until it started raining again.

Luke and Ryan were ecstatic. They spilled out their candy, and were overwhelmed by the sheer volume, not to mention the different "types" of treats.

"Wow! Look at this!" said Ryan, holding up some Chuckles, which I'm sure he'd never seen before.

"Yeah, look at this!" said Luke, holding up a giant Kit-Kat bar.

Ryan gulped, "Hey, I didn't get that."

And then the trading began . . . and the weeping . . . and the crying.

Matt stepped in. He said it was time for dinner.

The next morning, when Luke and Ryan awoke, they begged for some more candy. Matt said it was up in the cupboard, where they couldn't reach it, and they could have one piece—one piece—after dinner.

A week later, we visited Matt's house. I asked him how the candy was going. He said the twins forgot about it. And that was that.

CHAPTER 13

It was over a year now since I had my stroke, and I was getting on really well. My right leg was getting stronger. I only wore my leg brace a couple of times a week, and I was still getting out and walking a mile. It was still warm then, but it was getting cooler, and I had to find someplace to go. My right arm had no movement in it, and it moved up only when I forced it too.

A former student from Texas made me try a chiropractor for work with acupuncture, and I started that way back when I was in therapy. He said it was best to start when I was still within a year. Here's the dope about the acupuncture.

Lindy was suggested to me by Mary Lou Hess. I'd never met her, but I knew her husband well. Her husband, John, was the head basketball coach at Prospect High School, and one of my favorite students of all time. He was in my homeroom for four years, and in three or four of my classes. To say we admired each other would be an understatement.

I liked her the minute I saw her. She talked to me for a half-hour, making sure I understood what she was going to do, and how, after a while, it would help my right foot and arm. She explained the pins that would be stuck in both my legs, both my arms, and even in my head. I had never felt the pins before, so this was brand new. I finally said, "Go ahead."

So, the pins were stuck in. Some of them hurt more than others. Some of them really hurt, but after a while they settled down, and I was able to sleep. She left me in a pitch-dark room with "mood" music on. I was on my back and found it easy to sleep. I thought about many things, how this would eventually make me all better, and I really didn't mind the peacefulness of it all.

Lindy came in about halfway through, woke me up, and adjusted the pins. She would always ask me how I

76

was doing, how I felt, and everything about my life. As the months went on, I would see her three times a week, and I became close to her. She even invited us over for dinner and to meet her children. We bought her a nice gift for Christmas.

But, the gist of it was: the acupuncture was really not helping. As we plowed into January, I decided to not see her anymore. It was a tough decision. I can say now that acupuncture was not for me. And I don't blame Lindy. She did all she could do. It was just a block in my brain. I was trying to do anything I could do to heal my stroke, and the truth of it was acupuncture wasn't going to work.

****

As I said before, I had to find someplace to walk when the winter became cold. That place was the Wheeling Park District. Joani and I checked it out on November 12th, and we found out it only cost ten dollars for a year of walking.

We smiled for our photos, which were displayed on our tags. We had to wear our tags every time we walked; otherwise, there were basically no limits.

The track was up and above the basketball courts, which were twice a week used for racquetball. It was a narrow circle. Six and a half times around meant you walked a half-mile. Thirteen times around meant you walked for a mile. So you didn't get dizzy or wear the track out, it was one way four times a week, and the other way three times a week. You had to walk closest to the rail at all times when you weren't passing or running. Since I walked so slowly—I didn't pass anyone but an old lady—I clung to the railing.

I started to feel good, and we walked every chance we got. I even got to drive the car over to the park. Joani sat still and let me drive. We walked close to five times a week, mostly in the morning. Sometimes I walked with my leg brace, sometimes without. It was crowded in the morning when we went over about ten-thirty.

I felt tired when I walked a mile. I would sit and watch Joani finish up, usually walking twenty-six laps, or two miles. She would always chat with somebody, and the topic would usually turn to me.

A casual observer, who had noticed her come in with me, would say, "That's your husband, isn't he? I've noticed that he's had a stroke. How's he doing?"

Joani would answer, "That's my husband, all right. He had a stroke a year ago August. His right side's paralyzed, and he can't talk very well. But, he's doing well. He's learning to talk again, and, as you can see, he's walking quite well. His right arm doesn't move."

"That's good. God bless him. If you don't mind me asking, how old is he?"

"He's sixty-three. A bit young for having a stroke."

It didn't take long for me to learn the names of the people. The same people would come every day about the same time, and, as they were mostly old, they were never shy about saying something encouraging. "Keep walking, young man."

I soon realized that I was a boon to them. The more they saw me walking, the more they were encouraged to keep on coming.

I soon got tired of the crowd in the morning, and started to try the afternoon. There was virtually nobody there, which meant for no noise. Thankfully, there were no pick-up basketball games down below, and only racquetball on Tuesdays and Thursdays. By staying within myself, and watching what I ate, I was able to keep my weight down—or at least normal. I switched back and forth between mornings and afternoons, whatever was best for Joani.

This year, Joy, Stephen, and Charlotte would be spending Thanksgiving at our house, and Christmas at Stephen's parents' house. They arrived on Tuesday, and set up Christmas cookies for early Thanksgiving. Joy was in charge of the cookies; she had done this before.

Matt, Becki, Luke, and Ryan arrived, and Joy told them what to do. We all had a blast! So many shapes and sizes of cookies there were, all decorated nicely. There were reindeer and snowmen, stars and candy canes. Joy let them decorate with so many different colors that they looked glorious while they sat on the freezer, all spread out and super-sized. Joy got an A+ for her leadership.

I drove (left-handed) over with Stephen to pick up my mom, and surprised her. I felt more normal than I ever did before.

The Thanksgiving meal was as it should be: turkey, stuffing, mashed potatoes, sweet potatoes, gravy, green beans, corn, rolls, and a choice of pie for dessert, pumpkin or pecan. A family tradition was held every Thanksgiving right before our meal. It was the dry corn kernels, to be dumped in a basket that was passed around to each person, who would say whatever it was that they were thankful for. Everybody chose three kernels. I was most thankful for what I had gained from the stroke, and whom I was grateful for in helping me to cope with it, my wife Joani. It was still under a year and a half since I'd had the stroke.

The fact that Stephen was in the house meant that we didn't have to call the neighbors over to carry up the heavy boxes and set up the Christmas tree and village. In fact, I had made up my mind that I was ready to hang the ornaments where they go and set up the village. I was much stronger a year later, and I was going to do it!

After Stephen got the tree in position, "No, back a little! To the side a little! Turn it around so that side's facing out!" I was ready to decorate it the way it should be. You can understand now how my obsessive-compulsive disorder made me the worst person in the world a son or daughter would want to spend time with on a family project.

My daughter Joy would start out helping me hang the ornaments each year with, "How does that look, daddy?"

"It looks great. But it would look better over here!"

Thus, I would end up doing it by myself. Back in the day before we had a tree with multi-colored lights already set in place, I would end up doing the lights by myself too. I know, I know, it was a typical daddy-daughter time together, but I was just plain stupid to see it that way. I could always do everything better myself. That was one thing the stroke taught me: sometimes it's better to do things as a group—or at least have somebody, like the kind-as-can-be neighbors, help me with something.

Our neighborhood was a tinsel-town treat. Every house would decorate with something big, and sightseers would clamor, car after car, to see the neighborhood. Once, when I was at a Christmas party held by Bill and Georgette Witt, I decided to fool the cars going by. I perched myself on the lawn as an audio-animatronics robot and acted out my scene. The laughter from inside the house practically cancelled out the car noise.

I worried about falling from the sky, and therefore never let the kids climb onto the roof, or at least that's what I said. I did let Matt up once, and maybe Joy, and have the pictures to show people. But, for the most part, I did it by myself. It took several days.

I strung the hooks along the top gutter of the roof; then I placed the lights onto them, two strings of twenty-five for a grand total of fifty. Then, I strung another fifty lights over the peak on the top of the living room and along the bottom gutter, and met them with twenty-five lights over the peak of the garage. They were big lights, 125 in all. But, that was only part of the lights display.

The small, Italian lights, 2,900 in all, decorated my bushes to the left and right of my front, wooden door. To the left and on the end of my series of bushes rested a tall evergreen. It held 2,000 of the lights. I started on top of the roof and worked my way down, using a tall pole to hang up the middle ones.

Finally, I pieced together a nativity scene with a blue spotlight, and three letters that spelled out J-O-Y with a red spotlight. (Matt always complained that I would only show one of my children. He got his M-A-T-T next to J-O-Y in 2014, a gift from Mr. Moon.) By the way, Mr. Moon joined in the Christmas festival, even though he was Jewish; he hung up a very large peace sign on the top roof of his house.

All in all, there were so many cords that they almost overwhelmed the right part of the porch, behind the old wooden bench, perched one on top of the other. Matt Crost, a neighbor, laughed so hard and referred to my house as Chevy Chase's Christmas Vacation.

I stopped putting the lights on the roof when we got a new one compliments of our insurance company, Liberty Mutual, when our house was shelled by golf-ball sized hail one summer. They paid for the new siding too. Joy came home from college one year and said, "Dad, how come you didn't put up the Christmas lights on the roof?"

I answered, "Joy, we stopped doing that three years ago."

Anyway, I did what I said I'd do. I straightened out the Christmas tree branches and hung the ornaments up one by one. My leg would start to hurt, and I'd finally have to give up and sit down. The rest would only last about ten minutes or so, and then I'd be able to continue.

The nice thing about this tree, since we'd given all the kids' ornaments to them, was that it sat really well in the corner. Thus, we had only about two-thirds of the tree to decorate. I placed all the ornaments on in about three hours. I went to bed that night feeling good about what I had accomplished.

The next morning when I woke up, I knew I had to set up the Christmas village. And I knew how I had to do it.

The ottomans that sat below the village and prevented one from seeing all the cords were the perfect perch for my bottom. The only other way I could do it was to kneel down, and I wouldn't have lasted more than five minutes that way. Seated on one of the ottomans, I was able to work, for about two hours, neatly setting up the Christmas village. A year ago, I would have thought I could never do this again. But, bit-by-bit, I was conquering my stroke.

CHAPTER 14

This winter was horrendous. I was forced to walk indoors because there was too much snow at any time outside. If you've ever had a stroke, you know what it's like to have to walk. Try as you might, you favor one leg over the other because you feel like your bad leg is going to crumble down. Kyle would always say, "You're not going to collapse. Your right leg will hold you up. Just lean on it."

Sounds good. But what if you're wrong? So, I walked with the left leg taking all of the weight, a mile each day. It wasn't long before I had troubles with my IT band.

Joani would say, "You need to warm up more."

So, I'd take time and warm up both before and during my walk.

She would say, "You don't have to walk a mile. And you don't have to do it so fast."

I'd argue, "Well, what's the use of coming over here and trying to walk if I'm not going to do better?" This was one of my handicaps. I'd try to do better even if it was hurting me.

Finally, sometime in February, we went in to see Dr. Marinko. I hoped he would not be sending me back to Kyle; I knew how he always said, "Wow, this IT band is tight. Let's see if we can loosen it up." And the pain would begin.

My new book *Abner's Story* had come out in December, and I presented the novel to Dr. Marinko. He was ecstatic, even though I knew he was not going to read it. I also gave him an article written by Denise Fleischer for the Wheeling Journal about my story. And she also wrote about the stroke.

"Well, let's see what's wrong."

He pried it and pushed it, and pretty soon he came out with the exact diagnosis I had predicted. "It's the IT band. I suggest you take about a month or two of rehab. Is there a place you'd rather go?"

Joani suggested Athletico. She knew Sarah, and she knew she could help me. That sounded good to me. Any place but Kyle's dungeon.

Joani found out that Sarah only worked part-time. But she knew Brooke, whom she immediately recommended. I met her on the first day, and she took me inside a curtain and proceeded to learn all about my ailments. She suggested three times a week, all of which would be paid for by my insurance company.

And, the fun began. Monday, Wednesday, Friday, I limped over to Athletico, where Brooke would work on me. She would lay me down on a bed that was too narrow, heat me up so my leg would be warm, and proceed to work me over. Brooke was a female, so she didn't do it as hard as Kyle. I was reminded of this once when she was absent, and I had a rough male. He, with a smile in his eyes, worked me over like a rag doll; I bit the pillow, so I could keep from crying.

Finally, as the winter wore down, Brooke told me I could walk on those days when I wasn't with her. "Now," she said, "go slow. And if you feel any pain, especially in your IT band, stop and warm up a little or walk slowly the whole way. And, remember, don't do a mile. A half-mile is where you want to start. I'd say a half-mile is all you want to do."

It worked. Brooke released me as spring was coming, and I felt good about walking the half-mile. I could walk all the time outside and didn't have to worry about the Wheeling Park District. It may have been that I was turning too much or I was walking too fast. Or maybe it was just the stroke. Kyle once told me that the people with their right side paralyzed were more cautious. He said it was just that way. So, it was bad enough to have a stroke. Now I was more cautious. Oh, brother.

****

One day in early February, Mr. Moon stopped by for an unexpected visit. "Do you want to see a sporting event?"

I had not seen, I thought, the Cubs, White Sox, Bears, Bulls, or Blackhawks since the stroke. The vast crowds, the walk down the aisles, and the sitting up and down would be extremely dangerous. I thought of the last time I had seen a sporting event. May, 2012—the Cubs versus the Los Angeles Dodgers. With Mr. Moon and Denny McSherry. It was cold as can be.

I got the tickets—freebies, of course. And I was to drive. Mr. Moon said to take Euclid instead of Dundee Road; to eat Subway instead of buying the park treats; and to turn down the heat. Funny fellow.

We were cold sitting in what used to be called the grandstands. Denny McSherry wasn't wearing any coat, and he was dressed in shorts. He stood once with his back shielded from the wind up against the grandstand poles, which usually kept one from seeing the game. Mr. Moon and I were laughing hysterically. The Cubs were winning—no, I'm not making this up—so we went home early. We heard the last out as we pulled into Mr. Moon's driveway.

"Yahoo, Cubs win!" I said. And that was the last time I saw a sports team live. If you could call the Cubs a "sports team."

Before I could answer, Mr. Moon said, "I'll pick you up Friday at 4:00. It's a Bulls' game."

"Who are they playing?"

"I don't know. Does it matter?"

"I guess not."

I was talked into flying down the freeway to the United Center by Mr. Moon, in spite of my reluctance to go. Oh, well.

We left at 4:00, and drove down through the rush-hour traffic. It was mostly light, although the sun was setting. It was good to see the city again. Off the expressway, through the winding city streets, onto Madison Avenue.

"Gimme the handicap sticker."

"Here it is," I said, with the slightest bit of fear welling up inside of me.

Mr. Moon drove into the rich people's parking places, and parked right by the Michael Jordan statue, as close as you could get to the building without being in it. These were $40.00 parking places.

"Here, look at these."

"Oh, we're playing the Dallas Mavericks."

"Not that. The price of each of those tickets." Mr. Moon had never paid for anything in his life. The price of each of those tickets was $900.00. They belonged to his brother-in-law.

I was impressed, although he's taken me several times to these seats.

"They're not the front row seats (the seats where you've got to watch your legs). They're in the second row."

Passing all the people lined up to take snapshots with Michael Jordan, we were into the United Center in a stone's throw. Now, I offered to buy Mr. Moon his dinner; it was the least I could do. Twenty dollars later, we had two hot dogs and two Cokes. We moved over to the stand-up tables, and I vowed to put mustard on my hot dog. It was next to impossible to pour mustard with my one good hand. This was one of the tasks that I had to get used to, accepting help where I couldn't do it myself. It was always something easy to do, and I had to make up my mind to let it be done. Mr. Moon smiled at me. He let me know by that smile that he was willing to let me try it myself, but then, when I gave up, he was there to do it for me.

He took me to the long aisle leading down to our seats. There were no handrails, and he heard me say, "No way!"

Mr. Moon was ready. He said, "I just wanted to see if you could do it. We'll take the elevator."

The elevator led us down to the basement, where we were all alone except for the usher that led us down there. We walked a little bit, and Mr. Moon shouted out when he saw the hockey goalies.

"Sweet!" I was getting into it now.

The usher said, "And here's your private bathroom if you have to go during the game." Up one more ramp. "And here are your seats."

I only had to go up one step. I liked to look at the people's faces when they saw me, especially climbing up the stairs. They were looking at me with pathetic faces, saying to themselves, "Oh, look at that poor man." I appreciate a man—or woman—

opening a door for me, or slowing down to let me pass by. They're probably saying, "There, but for the grace of God, go I."

We sat down, and began to look around. Mr. Moon, upon removing his coat, had a Bulls' t-shirt on; I forgot to wear my Bulls' 1966 black-with-red-design sweatshirt. I thought it was okay to wear the Blackhawks' "sweater." They were winning more often. The crowd was jacked up. It was a typical United Center audience.

Just as the game was supposed to start, a large man and his family tried to squeeze past me. I got up to my feet as best I could, and leaned backward. He said, "Excuse me, sir." It was Jesse Jackson. Following him was all his family, including Sandi Jackson, who was going to be off to jail as soon as her husband got out. She brushed her diamond ring past me, and I can say it was Gargantuan. I leaned toward Mr. Moon and said, "At least we know what we paid for." He laughed.

The Bulls won, and scoring just over 100 points, the audience was treated to Big Macs, as long as we were willing to stop at the local McDonald's. Mr. Moon picked up a discarded ticket stub, so my wife could enjoy one too. Overall, I enjoyed the evening, but I was working on a little surprise of my own.

Randy Davis, a lawyer, went to my church. He had Bulls' tickets for March 22nd. And he gave them to me. "You're going to love these. First of all, you have dinner and then some of the richest desserts you'll ever taste. Most people don't know these seats are there."

I assumed these were like the rich people seats, where one eats two or three things, and then everybody feasts on desserts. I couldn't have been more wrong.

March 22nd happened to be Susan Moon's birthday. We were in a good mood, not knowing quite what to expect. We parked in the privileged zone with the handicap sticker, which meant we just had to cross the street and then we were in the building. We took the elevator up to the fourth floor.

These Bulls' tickets were called Club Boxes, and they did not have the price listed on any of these. We were playing the 76ers, who had lost 22 in a row, but that didn't make any difference at all.

We walked a ways and then opened the door to the Club Boxes. A neat row of tables sat almost empty. They were embroidered with fancy white tablecloths and silverware. A lady who was to be our hostess came right up to meet us, and she showed us our seats, which were right by the table. They were not like any other boxes; they were four seats, two in the front and two in the back.

Then, the hostess said, "Your meal is right over there. The prime dinner meal is set out through the first half only. The desserts and the bar are open all night. You can have as much as you like. I'll leave you to eat your dinner. May I get you a drink? Beer, wine, a mixed drink, pop?"

"Coke," we muttered.

Rather mesmerized, we walked over to the table, which were really two tables set up like a buffet. The first table had all the main dishes on it: prime rib, turkey, ham, chicken, mixed salad, potatoes, and asparagus. The second table had all the desserts and some other culinary delights on it: regular hot dogs, Polish dogs, boxes of popcorn, cheese cake, brownies, pies, and different kinds of cookies. The dogs had every kind of relish imaginable.

We just stood, in shock, looking at the buffet line. Mr. Moon said it best: "I've been to the United Center many times. And I didn't know this place existed."

We shook our heads in unison.

We filled our plates and headed to our table. Sure enough, our Cokes were there, as was water. It was only 6:00, so we had plenty of time to eat. And, let's face it, we had the whole first half to load up. After eating dinner, we decided to move to our seats. First, we had to use the bathroom; it was private, much like the one downstairs. Who said it was an inconvenience to have a stroke?

In our boxes, the wives sat in front of us, the husbands in the back. We were looking at the court from behind the backstop, rather high up. But we weren't complaining.

The game started. And the hostess brought us everything we could imagine, and then some: hot dogs, Polish dogs, some dessert, and—oh, yes—several boxes of popcorn with three or four Cokes. (Mr. Moon also had a Ginger Ale.)

Mr. Moon sat eating his popcorn in a spell of delight, turned to me and said, "You've impressed me. And I don't think I've ever said that before."

When the husbands got up to get some more food, Susan Moon laughed because there were so many spilled pieces of popcorn on Mr. Moon's chair, none on mine. She said, "Which one of you had the stroke?"

We had mentioned, in private, to the hostess that it was Susan Moon's birthday. Sure enough, she came with a brownie decorated with, "Happy Birthday, Susan!" It was also Benny the Bull's birthday.

The Bulls won. In other words, who cared? It was the ambiance of a beautiful dinner with great friends that made the night. We tipped the hostess, and hung around until most of the people had gone. It was a great night!

CHAPTER 15

It was to be a wild weekend in March. My son Matt had gotten us tickets and given them to me on Christmas. We were going to see live on stage Elvis Presley, Johnny Cash, Carl Perkins, and Jerry Lee Lewis in *Million Dollar Quartet*. It was going to be one rock concert filled with the story of what went on that night in 1956.

Matt picked me up in mid-afternoon, and we were on our way. The freeway was empty, and we didn't hit any snags until we hit those potholes on the side streets. It had been a rough winter; the potholes screamed as our car went down into them.

Matt, trying to avoid them, said, "Man-alive! Are these potholes ever deep?"

I couldn't believe it. It had been a terrible winter, filled with snow, ice, and driver's curses. But, this was too much. Some of the potholes would have swallowed our car if we had hit them. It took us as long to navigate the side streets as it did to fly down the freeway.

Finally, we arrived at the Apollo Theatre. Matt backed in the car, and he told me to watch it as I got out. There was snow all over the parking lot; I had to walk maybe thirty feet. I did so, without suffering a fall like I did in 2012. This was the first time I'd been in this theatre, and it was quite small.

A bit later, we were let into the theatre, and it was a long way up to our seats.

"Just relax," Matt said. "You can make it. Here, give me your hand."

I had learned over the course of walking that I could make it just about anywhere; all I needed was to take somebody's hand so I wouldn't fall. I relaxed, and, with everybody watching me,

I made it to my seat. Easy, I thought. What about going down after the show?

I am a bit of a worrywart, and so I thought about this until the show started. And then I quickly forgot it.

The Master of Ceremonies announced, "Ladies and gentlemen, this show will last about an hour and a half. There will be no intermission. So, sit back and enjoy the presentation."

They started with Carl Perkins' "Blue Suede Shoes," and, with their brilliant acting, carried us along for the ride. It was made known to the audience that this was the only time the foursome had been together, and that Elvis was not going to sign a new contract with Sun Records. He was on his way to a sweeter deal with a national record company, RCA.

The music was out-a-sight. When you think about the four kids forming a band back then, it was a magic night. Jerry Lee Lewis was the youngest member of this little quartet in 1956, but he brought along a whole lot of showmanship. We were encouraged to stand up and sing along with the band on the last number. This was very apropos for me. My legs would get stiff when I sat for an hour or more, and this gave me the flexibility to move, which I did.

Matt said, as the applause died down, "Let's try the back way. There's a staircase back there. I'm sure you can make it."

I walked up two steps, slightly easier than if I'd gone downstairs. I made it faster than I would have thought possible. I held onto the rail and just put one foot in front of the other, and I was down. It wasn't until I thought about it that I realized I had gone down with the left foot first—in other words, the wrong way. Kyle would have been proud of me.

I walked slowly to the car. We dodged the potholes as we talked enthusiastically about the play. Finally, I brought up a subject that I was hesitant to talk about.

"Matt," I said, "It's been a year and a half since I had the stroke. What I want to know is, can you understand me?" This speech problem was my biggest concern. I wanted to know if I could, for the most part, be understood.

Matt hesitated. "Dad, I can understand you just fine. You've come a long way. Don't worry about it. You don't talk like you used to, but I can understand you. I'll ask you if I don't comprehend you."

Matt and Joy were both angels. Matt had taken me to my first Notre Dame game, an upset loss to Boston College because they were 8-0 at the time. And he had surprised me with a trip downtown for a special dinner. I thought, what a boy, now he's making up for all those Cubs' games I took him to. What I didn't know is that he was surprising me with Paul McCartney tickets at the United Center.

And now, he was doing what he always did—telling the truth. I was getting better, and he was proud of me. I couldn't have asked for anything else.

****

It was spring. My new book *Abner's Story* was out, and I was starting to get places to read it. Terri Campbell, the Prospect Heights Public Library woman who oversaw the adult program, signed me up to share my book with the public. I told her I would be happy to do so.

My wife helped me reach the imminent conclusion. I would tell stories about the novel; she would read the three short passages that I would help her pick out. Her reasoning was simple: I could not read fast enough to put the proper diction on the key words or phrases. She was an expert reader, a former high school Individual Speech Events champion in Radio Speaking. I would tell them about my story; she would read to them the events. A perfect duo!

I spent the week before emailing every Facebook follower and reaching out to all my friends, past and present. I knew so many of my friends had previously bought the book, and so many colleagues had other things to do, that it'd only be about forty or fifty that would show up. If I was lucky!

My last showing was a sit-down affair, the re-opening of the Arlington Heights Memorial Library with some new sections for people to browse through. I was chosen, along with fourteen local authors, by Linda Mulford to sit, sell, and sign my first two novels (my third one wasn't due out for a few months yet). It was a field day.

I talked to many people, told them both books were available in the library, and sold eighteen novels, much more than any of the other authors. I was getting rather good with my left hand; signing autographs wasn't that hard.

The build-up to the presentation was nerve-wracking. Just because I'd been a teacher for so many years didn't mean I didn't get nervous. We took off an hour ahead of time, the script ready to go. At least I didn't have to spend so many hours reading; that was Joani's job.

We arrived at the library at 6:00; the presentation started at 7:00. We were able to get everything set up before the people arrived. There were snacks on a table in the back, store-bought cookies. I was too nervous to eat two—or three—now, but wait until this show was over.

The people came. My mom, my neighbors, some friends; it was great! Terri Campbell introduced us, and I started the same way I had started at the schools, with a declaration that I had suffered a stroke. This, I felt, put everybody at ease, and I asked for questions.

My mom asked, "What about the cover?"

"Well," I answered, "the cover, which is of Wrigley Field during the height of a Cubs' game, almost never was published. I spent two hours going through these pictures, and finally I picked out this one, which looked great. I called my publisher, and she said we couldn't use it. Then, within a week, she called me and said it was all right. Anyway, it's a magnificent cover."

"Any other questions? No. Well, I suppose you're waiting to hear the novel read. Let me introduce my wife Joani, who will read a section from Chapter 1. But I'll be back. So, think of some more questions."

Joani began reading. She was super, just like I'd expected her to be. She read every word with the proper pace, diction, and the excitement in her voice that caused some people to want to buy a book. The night went on like that.

More questions were asked, and then suddenly, the presentation was over. People came up and met me, Joani sold, and I autographed books. It was a wonderful night. Oh, by the way, I feasted on three cookies to end the evening.

****

Dennis Olenik lived an hour and fifteen minutes away. His wife, Muriel, had to come back to their old church to work with women on the second Wednesday of every month, so Dennis came along to keep her company. The real reason he came back was to visit me.

Of all the people that lived so far away and came to visit me, Dennis was the most consistent, the former head librarian at John Hersey High School. He would usually bring his own lunch, sit with me for two hours, and see how I was progressing.

"Well, how are you doing?"

"Fine. I'm doing just fine."

I could tell it did him good to see how I was getting along. He was pleased to see I was walking at least a half-mile and getting out to see the plays and the Bulls. He could tell I was getting back to my own self, and we were both happy to see it.

"I've been reading these novels," I said, because I knew mention of books always made him sit up and pay attention. "*Sycamore Row* by John Grisham. Do you ever read any books by Grisham? They're the best."

"Yeah, I do. But I've got a non-fiction narrative that's bound to make you happy."

He reached into his bag and produced a book that I'd never heard of: *One Way Uphill Only*. It was 300 pages.

"Let me explain. This is the narrative of Palatine High School's cross-country state championship. My grandson Timmy Johnson was one of the five runners."

"Oh, wow! Who's the author?"

"Chris Quick is the author and the coach. He's also taught Advanced Placement English Language and Composition. You'll love the book."

So, there I had it. Palatine's first state championship. And it was fun to read, especially since I've known Timmy Johnson since he was born.

Dennis had challenged me. I couldn't wait until I saw him again.

CHAPTER 16

One day in March, Denny McSherry called me up. "Hey, you want to go with me to the Fox Lake Library to hear Michael Osacky talk about baseball cards? He's also gonna price out two of your cards. What'dya say?"

Denny knew that this was one of my passions, although I hadn't collected a baseball card in seventeen years. I had a complete set of 1962 Topps, now more than fifty years old, an almost complete set of 1963 Topps, and a complete set, only 129 cards, of 1960 football cards. And that was just the icing on the cake.

I first thought of Denny. "You sure you want to do this? You'll be bored."

He laughed. "No, I won't be. I don't know anything about baseball cards. You know me, I can learn something new."

I was touched. He was doing this for me. "Okay, when will you pick me up?"

"I'll be in town for some errands. I'll pick you up around 11:00. We'll get a bite to eat; then we'll go see him. He starts at 2:00."

We were in the library shortly before he was to begin. I had brought along two of my Mickey Mantle All-Star cards to see what they would be worth. I knew the 1961 card was a 7th series card—hard to come by—and worth $500.00. (Series used to come out through the summer. The 7th series came out in September when most of the kids were back in school and had lost interest in baseball.)

Michael started talking. "Baseball cards were overproduced in the 1980's. That's why I only collect baseball cards up to 1980."

He was interesting to listen to, and he had a slide show to make his points clear. He was a professional writer, and he collected baseball cards with a passion. He had some of the oldest and most sought-after cards of the 19th century. He impressed me.

After he talked about forty minutes, he opened it up to questions, most of which I knew the answers to. Then, he called upon people to bring up their cards for an estimate. He talked for a time to each person, and then shared with the audience what each card was worth.

It was finally my turn. I limped my way up there, and sat down. I explained to him I used to be a card collector, and I stopped when my son reached seventeen and was just not interested any more.

He said, "Well, you've got two Mickey Mantle cards. Let's look at them. Ummm, the priciest one's got a bend in one corner. You see that?"

I hesitantly agreed with him. Is he for real? He took out his spyglass and looked hard at the card. He'd made up his mind.

He addressed the crowd. "This gentleman has got two Mickey Mantle All-Star cards. This one's fairly easy to come by; I'd say it's worth about $50.00. The other one's a 7th series, and it's worth about $175.00."

What?

Denny and I said good-bye and headed to the car.

I said, "He low-balled my card. It's worth at least $500.00. He's a real dealer."

The day was over. Or so I thought. Denny had picked up one of his cards; it had his email and address written on it. I said it would be worth it to send him my third book (*Abner's Story*) and see if he'd do a write-up about it.

I started by sending him an email congratulating him on his presentation and asking him whether he'd like an autographed copy of *Abner's Story*. He emailed me back and told me he would be happy to receive a copy. And then he volunteered to read the story and write a blog on *Parade* reviewing the story.

I waited over a month and then asked him if he had finished my novel. He said he was about halfway through it, and sent me some general questions to answer while we waited. The questions were all generic, so the first-time reader would not have the story ruined for him. Some of them were:

Q: "What is your inspiration for the book?"

A: "That was a compliment to my late uncle. When he was a senior at Evanston, he and a friend cut school to see what turned out to be the last World Series game that the Cubs would ever win. He bought a scorecard, and the Cubs won in 12 innings. I received that scorecard (Game 6) from my aunt when my uncle died. The strangest thing: there are only white players on the team. 1945 was a long time ago. I also thought it would be neat if there was a man around who remembered (in 2020) the last time the Cubs won a World Series."

Q: "What is something you have kept from all those dates at Wrigley Field?"

A: "I have scorecards that are neatly kept in pencil, which allows one who saw all those games to look back and remember the big plays."

Q: "What is your favorite chapter?"

A: "The last chapter. The book finally came together at that point. I thought it up lying in bed one night. It's the only chapter there isn't a manuscript for. I had to type it before I forgot."

Q: "Do you think the Cubs will ever win another World Series?"

A: "Well, we have been promised . . . (Ha. Ha.)"

And that was it. For a while. He eventually wrote me and told me he'd enjoyed the book. And he said, "The Parade post is up—now! I hope you enjoy it."

I followed his directions, and it wasn't long before I was face-to-face with the article. It was a sweet dream!

I emailed him and told him I liked it. I thanked him for doing it for me.

He emailed me back and said, "I'm glad you like it. If you ever decide to sell your old baseball cards, I'll give them a happy home."

****

I've always been a Cubs fan. And so, I finally got around to building the thousand-piece jigsaw puzzle of Wrigley Field. It was the test, actually, to see if I recovered from my stroke—mentally, that is. I worked on this for two or three hours each day. I started with the borders, and then worked myself in. It was a long and complicated process, and it often drew me to distraction.

Luke and Ryan had come to visit one day. Ryan was always kind when he directed his comments at me. "Oh, Pop-Pop, you're walking much better these days." or "Let me help you up (from your chair)." I had noticed he was getting stronger at building jigsaw puzzles, so he was invited in to see my Wrigley Field design. What Ryan did next, at five years old, was miraculous.

He looked the non-connected puzzle pieces over, and within five minutes, he had picked out three of them that fit perfectly. I stared at him in awe.

"I'm a master puzzle connector," he said. "I'm gonna grow up to be a puzzle builder."

He and Luke, during their fifth year, started to build Lego designs, such as rocket ships, police cars, and fire trucks. When I asked them, "Did you build this yourself?" they always answered, "Yes."

They inspired me to finish, which I finally did. It turned out to be a masterpiece. My old self, besides my ability to remember people's names and other direct objects, was at least back mentally.

So, it was with some hesitation that I met with Dave Truelsen, who offered me tickets to a White Sox-Yankees game.

"It'll really be fun. We'll ask a bunch of people to join us, and everyone will fit in my van. We'll meet downtown for dinner at around 5:00, and still make it in time for the opening pitch."

I said, "Yes. I've always wanted to get back and see a Major League baseball game." (I had made it to and from the Bulls' game, so why not?)

He picked me up between 3:00 and 3:30 pm. Included in the van were: Steve Oldham, Charlie Hess, Jim Pietrini, Dave, and me. We were to meet, at the restaurant, John Clarkson and Joe Vanella, who worked downtown, seven in all. The van ride was something else; it took us three hours, so the 5:00 time turned into a 6:00 time.

We ended up calling John Clarkson, and he ordered for all of us. The restaurant, Geo's, of Italian fame, was spoken highly of by Jim. And he was not mistaken. We were hungry, so we ate up some delicious Italian food, skipped dessert, and high-tailed it out of there by 6:30. We didn't want to be late for the game.

I determined not to forget the handicapped pass, so this let us into the zone right in front of U.S. Cellular Park (also known as new Comiskey Park).

Dave spoke, "I've never parked so close to the park. This is a first."

I have known Dave for years, and I never knew he was a Yankees fan. But there he was, all dressed up in his Yankee sweatshirt and cap. He had come to see Derek Jeter play his last time at the Cell.

We parked the van and went inside to the elevator. Jim was a White Sox fan, and had gotten the tickets for us. He was very proud of all of us coming to see the game with him. It was his time to show off the South Side of Chicago to us who live in the North Side suburbs.

I balked at the stairs. They led down to the seventh row, and there were at least thirty-five rows to climb down, with no handrails. Steve took my arm, and said, "I've got you. Take your time."

We were finally seated, in time to stand up for the National Anthem. We had made it in the nick of time. I looked over the ballpark and saw the rays of the sunlight just descending. I felt at home. Chris Sale took the mound for the first time since he'd come back from a minor injury; he was awesome.

The intriguing part of this ballgame was not Derek Jeter, it was Chris Sale's perfect game. The Sox took an early lead, and Chris took his perfect game until two outs in the sixth. He was removed shortly thereafter, and the applause was noisier than that for Derek Jeter.

But Derek and his boys weren't finished yet.

It was the top of the ninth, the Sox led 3-0, and we decided to beat the crowd and head for home. Hopefully, it wouldn't take us another three hours to get home. It was my worst part of the evening.

It was increasingly cold as the night wore on. I stood up, and immediately felt my legs weren't all there. I would need some time to get them right. Unfortunately, I didn't take the necessary time. I hesitated at the sheer number of stairs leading up, not the stroke victim's most favorite past time. Dave took my arm. I started my foolish walk up the concrete steps. I wasn't making it. I almost fell twice, the second time causing a fan, who was watching me (everybody was), to step up and say, "Oh, for crying out loud . . ."

He grabbed my other arm and helped me up the stairs. I didn't thank him, so wherever you are, thank you.

I was exhausted. The rest of the men watched the Yankees bat in the ninth as I headed toward the elevator, accompanied by Charlie and John. The Yankees came back, made the score 3-2, and had two men on base. The last man made an out, preserving Chris Sale's victory for him. I struggled all the way to the elevator, when the friends caught me and told me about the exciting last outs. Dave looked particularly depressed.

We said good-bye to Joe, whom everyone knew except me, and John hopped in the van. We were on our way home. Or so I thought. There was one last stop to be made. We pulled over to a stand-up food chain called Maxwell Street Depot, where the men had to have pork sandwiches. I was too pooped even to eat, which showed how pooped I was. So, I sat in the van.

Dave came back, ate his pork sandwich, and talked to me. He said Joe Vanella liked me, and said I was doing well. That was good to hear; it made me feel happy inside. If there's one thing I liked to hear, it was that I didn't make trouble for anyone.

We had a long trip to the Cell, I ate at a restaurant, and I almost fell going up the steps. But, overall, I had accomplished another huge item of my list. And my friends had not deserted me when I needed them most. I slept very well that night.

CHAPTER 17

The summer of 2014 went by fast. I walked many miles, a half-mile at a time. My legs were getting stronger, but I still could not lift my right arm. I talked better than ever. I could make it seem as if I could always talk, the diction was clear. In August, I passed the two-year mark. Anne invited me back for three of her classes, where I talked nonchalantly about revision of *Ten Again*. I wasn't afraid to face a class anymore.

It was into October. We were going to spend two weeks with Joy, or until her new baby came along. The first weekend, we were going to spend celebrating Joani's forty-fifth reunion from Taylor University. I showed up to church feeling as fit as ever, greeted people, and attended the worship service.

On the way home, I felt terrible. There was so much pain in my left groin, I thought I might pass out. I could only think I had walked too much and strained my IT band again. I went home and sat in my Lazy-Boy chair, and finally fell asleep. I felt much better when I woke up. This happened once in a while. I would walk too much, or stand too much, and my IT band would hurt for a day or so, and then go away. It was part of healing. I slept through the night, and I felt better come Monday.

That day, I had one or two bouts with pain, and that night was horrible. I twisted and turned, and the pain was excruciating. About 5:00 pm, when we were getting ready to leave for Bible study, the pain doubled me up again, and we decided to go to the Med Center. I knew one thing—it wasn't the appendix, which was on the right side.

They X-rayed me, and, after a while, the doctor came in. He was as sure as ever what it was. It was a kidney stone—to be precise, two kidney stones. They were moving down in the left tube trying to get into the bladder. When they stood still, there was no pain; when they moved, there was ultra-pain. So, that's what it was. That made sense, although it seemed rather unfair that a man who had a stroke would have to go through this. I remembered the story of men having kidney stones, and the only way to pass them was through urinating. There was one story about a man on the way to the bathroom. He screamed, passed out, and broke his leg. Oh, boy.

The doctor told me to drink at least ten to twelve glasses of water a day. This would keep me peeing, and the kidney stones would soon pass out. He told me there was a rather large kidney stone in my right kidney, but that might never come out. Or if it did, we could deal with it then.

Well, the next few weeks were misery. My son Matt came over to watch the Notre Dame game that Saturday, and I rushed to the bathroom every few seconds, it seemed. We decided we would skip church on Sunday, because you never knew when the pain would hit me.

On Monday, we went to the urologist.

"This never comes out," I said. "The other doctor said it would be out in two to three days."

"It sometimes takes time. If you can get by on Aleve or Advil, you're probably better off. Don't take all those relaxing pills."

"You don't understand," said Joani. "We have to go back for my forty-fifth reunion on Friday. If he doesn't pass them, then we'll not be able to go."

"Keep drinking water. You'll be able to go."

Thursday came. I was still having pain, and I had to go to the bathroom every hour or so. We went back to the urologist, and he gave me some relaxing pills to help me not go to the bathroom as often. Wait, didn't he say not to take all those relaxing pills?

"He'll be all right. Go to your reunion."

Sure, he didn't have to stop ten times to Taylor in a four-hour drive.

Well, God must have wanted Joani to enjoy her reunion, because the next day, Friday, I was as good as new. I took the relaxing pills just to be able to say I was taking them, and they worked like magic. As far as I could tell, the kidney stones had finally passed.

The reunion was a blessing—for Joani. She was able to catch up with all her friends, some of whom she hadn't seen for forty-five years. And then there was good-old Diane and Steve Oldham, whom we saw every day. There was food both Friday night and Saturday noon/night, and I was able to eat again, so it was a blessing for me as well. Saturday night we had brisket made by an original chef at the President's house. It was to die for.

On Sunday, we made our way to Joy's condo. It was a pleasant two-and-a-half-hour trip through the Indiana cornfields.

"Did you have a good time?" I asked.

"Oh, it was beautiful. I was really glad we were able to go. And I'm so happy you're feeling all right. Now, be quiet, so we can hear the story." (It was one of those audio novels. It made it easy to mark the miles by, not so easy to talk.)

****

Joy was miserable. She itched all over, and the baby was likely to come out at any time. She had a week to finish, and then her fall break would come, and she'd be off for a week. (She had this fall break because her semester started on August 4th.)

We spent that week getting ready for the baby's delivery— Stephen and Joy did not want to know whether it was a boy or girl. We bought diapers, and some clothes for either sex. We came that year for Charlotte's second birthday, and she was getting to like us.

October 25th came and went. It was my mom's 93rd birthday, and it was also the due date for the new baby.

When we went home on Wednesday night to our handicapped shower in our hotel room just one minute away, these were Stephen's instructions: "I'll call you. Leave Mike; he's useless anyway." (Thanks, Stev-o.) "You'll come and watch Charlotte. We'll call you when the baby's born."

Well, the first call came about 11:00. "You stay here. I'll call you when I know anything."

I was glad I didn't have to leave. The World Series—the San Francisco Giants against the Kansas City Royals—was in the next-to-last inning. The Giants were trying to claim their third World Series in the last five years. Even though the game was in Kansas City, Madison Bumgarner was too tough for them. The Giants were victorious. I watched the celebration, and then I nodded off to sleep.

I awoke at around 7:00. Joani hadn't called yet, so I assumed the baby hadn't been born yet—poor Joy. Just then, the phone rang.

"Hello."

"Guess what?" said Joani. "The baby was born at 12:30. She gave birth in one and a half hours."

"Uh, what's the sex?"

"Oh, didn't I tell you that? I'm sorry. It's a boy. They named him Andrew Boston Becker. They were engaged in Boston, remember?"

"Yeah, I remember. Is Andrew healthy?"

"Yes. He's healthy."

We went to see him that morning. He was cute. His chubby cheeks were immense. Charlotte saw him for the first time, and she fell in love with him right away. Lying at home—he was naked, getting his diaper changed—Charlotte would peruse him up and down, and tell him how much she loved him.

"I love you, Andrew. I love your eyes, your ears, your cheeks, your chin, your stomach, your penis, your legs, and your toes."

Well, the first time Stephen and Joy heard her say that she loved his penis, they laughed so hard that they almost croaked.

I got to hold him. Stephen set him down in the crook of my left arm. Looking at Andrew, I understood why God kept me alive. Joani took a picture of us both—it was his birthday, October 30, 2014.

It was supposed to be nasty the next day. We decided to go home—after all, we'd seen what we came to see. And two weeks was a long time.

Stephen chose to get Charlotte all dressed up in her costume because there was a pre-Halloween celebration right in the town of Oxford. All the townies would be giving out treats. Charlotte was to be a lion.

Charlotte came back to the hospital—she was not just a lion. She was the cutest-ever lion made for this earth. She had her picture taken wearing her costume with Andrew.

Stephen called us a couple of hours later. "She's sitting on the curb, eating her treats. I think we're done. What would you like for supper?"

I think Charlotte liked the idea of Halloween, even though she didn't understand it. You just walked up to a front door, mumbled trick-or-treat, and somebody said how cute you were and gave you candy.

We said good-bye to everyone the next day and left for Chicago. It was one of the worst days to pose as Halloween. We battled rain and snow for five hours, and finally stopped at McDonald's for lunch. I was feeling bad because I couldn't drive—Joani wouldn't let me drive on such bad days. When we came out of the McDonald's, our car was covered with snow. We brushed it off and continued on. Thankfully, it wasn't snowing back home; it was cold though, with a northwest wind that swept all the way down from Minnesota.

****

Ditka's. That was to be the eating spot for Thanksgiving. Joani was not happy with the idea, but since it was Stephen's and Joy's turn to visit his parents, she went along with it. I didn't care, as long as we kept everybody at peace, and there was enough turkey for me.

Matt told us that he and Becki would be taking Luke and Ryan downtown to see all the Christmas lights and the windows at Macy's—aka Marshall Field's. They would be spending two nights downtown, where they hoped to take in a museum.

We were to pick up my mom and meet everybody at Ditka's at 2:00. It was the end of an especially cold November. The restaurant was a third full at said time. But, if we'd only known how tasty it would be.

We sat up and out of the crowd, and the dinner lasted three hours. Joani had brought the boys some coloring books to keep their minds on other things, and that worked well. The twins talked about kindergarten—they were in their first year—and to show us what they had learned, they took turns counting to one hundred.

The dinner kept coming in droves. There was salad, turkey, stuffing, the best-ever sweet potatoes, vegetables, and, for dessert, your choice of pumpkin pie cheesecake or pecan pie. We ate until we were full.

The boys ate well, and they were on their best behavior. We said good-bye to them—always a hard task—and dropped my mom off.

"Well," said Joani, "I certainly take back everything I said about Ditka's. That was quite a meal."

"It was," I said.

And the best was yet to come.

Returning home, it was only 5:30. We had no clean-up, no dishes to wash, no backbreaking labor to haunt our moves for the next two hours. We simply sat down, turned on the television, and promptly fell asleep. It was a good Thanksgiving.

CHAPTER 18

It was a mild winter. (So far.) No snow fell in December, and I could walk every day. We had the family coming over on Christmas Eve, and there were more presents under the tree than I'd ever seen before. Stephen and Joy were supposed to come on the Monday before Christmas, but we were in for quite a surprise.

It was Sunday night; I was working at my computer, and Joani was sitting in the family room watching television. It was about 9:40. Suddenly, the doorbell rang.

"Who's that?" I mumbled, while starting to get up from our kitchen table.

"I don't know," said Joani.

She opened the door, gasped a short breath, and looked down on a baby. He was wide awake.

I was horrified. Here we were, parents to a newborn baby. But even in his car seat, he looked bigger than a freshly printed baby.

Joani called out in a surprised, but elated voice. "Oh, Andrew, you've come for Christmas."

Stephen, Joy, and Charlotte came out from behind the brick wall. "Surprise!" said Joy. "We raced to get here. We thought you would already be in bed."

"Not quite," said Joani. "We were going to bed in just about fifteen minutes."

We were, of course, thrilled to have them. They were early because our three closet friends—Glenn and Kathy, Emil and Patty, and Bill and Georgette, along with their kids—were invited for a dinner on Tuesday night, the 23rd. It was a smash.

Stephen and Joy were in charge of all the food, which consisted of Chicken Parmesan, Italian Sausage, and pasta noodles with a deep, red sauce to complement everything. Needless to say, we had leftovers for the next week.

Christmas Eve started with Stephen and Joy accompanying my mom, Joani, and me to church, and then we met the rest of the family back at my house to open presents and eat dinner.

The "clothing" presents were from Joani and me. Blackhawks' sweaters—we call them jerseys—for Luke and Ryan with Kane on one shirt and Toews on the other. (They went to their first game, and were even on television.) Little Andrew received his shirt, a Blackhawks' prototype. He wears it around the condo on Saturdays.

And Charlotte received her black baby doll. Stephen said he wanted his girl to be exposed to multi-cultural dolls. She came with a whole set of baby paraphernalia, including clothes, wipes, and a comb. Stephen was looking for the wipes the next day, and he asked Charlotte where they were. She said that she threw them away. I mean, that was what you'd do with used baby wipes.

On Christmas day, Joani, Joy, Charlotte, and Andrew went to Rockford to visit Joani's mom. She said it made her day. Joy called Stephen and asked him to prepare dinner. So, he did that, while I cleaned up the living room, including vacuuming.

In January, it remained snow-free, and although it turned a little bit colder, I was able to walk every day, including January 31st, Joy's birthday and Ernie Banks' funeral. Yes, the great one had passed away, and he was buried on what was to have been his 84th birthday.

The next day was the Super Bowl, the Seattle Seahawks versus the New England Patriots. We were to go to Mr. Moon's house, only two blocks away. It was snowing so hard when we woke up that morning that we couldn't go to church. It was still snowing at 5:00 p.m.

We sat at home and watched the Super Bowl, as did most people. It was the fifth-largest snowfall in Chicago's history: 19.5 inches. And it would stay with us through a record third-coldest February.

Now, it was by no means Boston, which was plowed under by a near record setting 100 inches through the entire winter.

But, it was Chicago. And as we sat through February and waited for the snow to melt, which it did some time in March, we were glad we received so many books for Christmas. I read seven by the end of February.

****

Well, that's it—my first two and a half years with my stroke. Let me summarize for you the good and the bad of having such a stroke. What's the good part?

It's true that Joani's dad, Larry, died from a massive stroke in 1998. However, I still didn't see strokes as something I had to worry about. I didn't realize how many people died from having strokes. And, like I said before, basically everybody who knew me was surprised by me having gone down with such a severe stroke, one that the doctors still can't give me a reason for. So, I didn't die, for which I am eternally grateful.

I can do pretty much everything I did before. My right foot and right hand will go into spasms whenever I'm stressed; I can't help that. I can't feel my right foot or my right hand; they're basically numb—paralyzed would be a better word. But, I can walk with my right leg anywhere and everywhere I want. I don't wear any braces for my leg or arm, and the right arm stays fairly loose most of the time. That may not seem like much, but it's better than being stuck in a wheelchair or with a cane. And I've never fallen since that time in October 2012, when I forgot to lock my wheelchair.

I can talk, and it wasn't so long ago when I couldn't do that. I didn't know, when a person had a certain kind of stroke, that they had to re-learn their speech pattern. But, looking back, there was a time when, resting in the hospital, I didn't think I'd be talking much. I've had to re-learn every word I knew, and I thank God for His help. That's the thing about a stroke: you have to learn new patterns of doing things, and it doesn't come easy. But the brain can do it; it's really a remarkable piece of machinery. I wish I could remember names—this used to be a gift of mine—and direct objects, though.

I can drive, although Joani doesn't let me very much. We gave my car, a 2003 Jeep, to Joy, for which she was very thankful. So, we only have one car, and Joani prefers I drive it with Mr. Moon. I'd like to point out that I've never had an accident since 1966, and I've covered many miles of driving.

Most of all, the good part is being able to be with my children, grandchildren, wife, mom, and all my good friends. My best friends have been there all the time for me, and I am thankful for that. I have never, in two and a half years, had a friend or someone I didn't know look down on me. They have opened doors for me and every other type of kindness you can think of.

And then there's Joani. She's always beside me, doing things. I sleep through the night, getting up just once to go to the bathroom. I use my cane—it's the only time I ever use it—to walk into the bathroom at night or in the morning. I shower myself, dry myself, and limp to the bed. (Just recently, in December 2014, we had the bathroom re-done to better fit a handicap person.) I sit on the bed and dress myself, although I can't wait for spring to come because I can wear shorts again, which are much easier to climb into than long pants. My shoes are double-knotted, so I can force both of them on. My socks, t-shirt, and sweatshirt are easily put on. Remember, there was a time when I could not put any of these on, and Joani had to give me a bath.

I walk—without a cane—back into the bathroom and comb my hair. Then, I go alone—Joani's already down on the main floor—down the long stairs, which it seems like only yesterday Joani and Kathy helped me do. I walk out any side of the house and down the basement stairs. It wasn't too long ago that I had to walk the first half backward, but then Dan and Chris put in a left handle so I could walk down the basement stairs forward. At least I won't fall.

I dust the whole house. At first, I had to sit down after each room because I was so tired. But now, I take the main floor one day and the upstairs the next, and I'm never out of breath.

I eat with my left hand. It's easy. And I haven't spilled once, not at home, not at a restaurant. I can make my own breakfast, lunch, or dinner, with some minor adjustments. It's easier to have Joani do it, but I can do it on my own when she's not home.

I'm always ready to go out to a movie, a play, a sporting event, or breakfast/lunch/dinner. And I can always walk. I can also write with my left hand, and Joani says she can actually read it. (Ha. Ha.) I have to go slowly, but it all works out in the end. Not like my scribbling on the blackboard all those years ago.

I'm typing my fourth book—with my left hand. I never thought I could do it, but I'm getting fast. Well, fast for me.

Now, what's the bad part?

I miss keeping up around the house. I always did everything, and that's a real bummer. Just once, I'd like to cut the lawn, trim the bushes or trees, put the bark mulch in place, or snow blow the driveway. I think about it all the time. Well, maybe not all the time.

There's a hoop on our driveway, and I would go out there on a summer's night and shoot baskets. Man, I really miss that. Thankfully, I don't play golf, or I'd miss that. I'm sixty-five now, so I would probably hurt myself playing baseball or football. I will let it be only wistful memories.

The one "love" I long for is my teaching. As I said before, I was about to enter my forty-first year of teaching when I had the stroke, and that called an end to that beautiful magic. There's hardly a night that goes by when I don't dream about teaching at John Hersey, although that's odd because I haven't taught there for ten tears. I suppose it's like an athlete who has a career-threatening injury, and after months of therapy, he or she is forced to quit. What do they do with the rest of their lives? Well, I've only got a handful of years left, and I did have forty years of teaching. That's a blessing. I've had the best life I could imagine, and what's wrong with that?

Finally, I'd like to thank my therapists—at Elk Grove, Wheeling, and Athletico—for keeping me positive and looking ahead. I owe a great deal to them, every one of them. There was a time when strokes—when you survived—could limit you, but not anymore. All strokes are different, and I don't know, if you've had one, what you're going through right now. But, look up. Tomorrow's going to be a better day.

I'd like to thank all my friends and my church people. I've had my life rejuvenated by you. And I'd like to thank my Lord Jesus Christ, who made all of this possible.

Most of all, I'd like to thank my ability to talk and not say things that don't make sense. Like the time I said "tane" for the brace that sat on my leg. Mr. Moon and I are still laughing about that one.

****

Joani and I are sitting watching television. It's one of those nights where the daytime temperature has reached the sixties, and spring is in the air. We have learned everything about us, and there's not much more to learn. I trust her explicitly. I don't know what I would have done without her.

We will be celebrating our thirty-ninth wedding anniversary July 10th, 2015. I suppose I've got to do something big for our fortieth. Oh, well, I'll think of something. At least my mind still works.

EPILOGUE

Joani went to hear a speaker whose husband suffered a major stroke, very near the time I had mine, March instead of August. It was particularly rough on Joani, because it brought back memories of those horrible times. Her husband was in the same rehabilitation place with the same doctor. She still got him into his wheelchair. Joani happened to see her after the speech, so she mentioned my stroke to her.

"Sisters-in-stroke," she said. "Is he still going to rehab?"

This was something my wife never considered, I having been out of rehab for nearly twenty months.

"We are going to see Dr. Marinko on Tuesday. Do you think I should ask?"

"By all means."

It was something I was keen on doing, so when Dr. Marinko wrote the order, I was actually looking forward to it.

I was on Medicare for the first time, and it was different. We only got to go three times a week for half days, 8:30–11:20. I would have physical and occupational therapy, but no speech therapy. It would last five weeks.

Most of the therapists had moved on; only Kyle and Sue would be my mentors. Of this, I couldn't have been more pleased. They both made me ecstatic by wearing ties on Tuesday, especially for me.

They decided they would work on things I couldn't do well, such as putting more weight on my right leg, and doing more with my right arm, such as carrying grocery items in a small bag. Jessica worked with me on this one. She determined that I had a "dead-man's grip" that I hung onto for dear life. Occasionally, I would let go after a long walk, and then I'd have to stop and tighten my grip. It worked though.

Rachel and Amy worked with me on holding jars steady and taking them, and everything else, out of a box. Most of these were done with my left hand, however. They had never seen anybody so fast though.

Allie worked with me on wearing a harness so I wouldn't fall and taking slow steps, putting more weight on my right leg.

Allison, a graduate from John Hersey High School whom I had never had in class before, played games with me, Yahtzee and Sequence, using my right hand. She devised a cone, which I could hold in my right hand to roll the dice. I beat everybody at the table, and I was known as the "King of all Games."

Sue was impressed with my left-handed writing, which she used with me to fill out my "Discharge Plan" on the last day. She said you could read it well.

Kyle was blown away by my strength and my endurance during my five-week stay. He worked on stretching my lower muscles out on my right leg once or twice a day. Man, did that hurt.

And he took me on my old favorite, the treadmill, without any strap-me-in and hold-me-down device. The only thing he connected was the red strap to my right side to allow the numbers, especially the time, to be shown on the treadmill. Then, he jacked it up and let it go.

I was moving along pretty good. And then, my right hand caught up with the red strap and jerked it out, which automatically stopped the machine, supposedly a safety device. I was thrown down on the treadmill going backwards. For the first time since October 2012, I fell. But it wasn't my fault.

I was still balanced on the treadmill; only my butt really hurt. All the therapists in the area gathered around me, and Kyle asked, "Are you all right?"

I answered with a grin, "Yes, I'm all right."

Kyle relaxed and said, "Boy, you almost had it. Your right leg and your left leg were in sync. You just missed the bar with your left hand."

I answered the only way I could. "Well, if you were able to think all that, why didn't you save me from falling?"

Oh, and I beat Kyle at bowling (139-128)—once, but that's enough.

I left, eternally grateful for what they had done. I supplied the staff with Fannie May candy, Sue with my third book, and Kyle with a set of golf balls that read simply SOX. I wrote in his thank you note, "Kyle, thank you so much for working with me—wait, that's your job, isn't it?"

Review Requested:
If you loved this book, would you please provide a review at Amazon.com?

Lightning Source UK Ltd.
Milton Keynes UK
UKHW040619211119
353970UK00001B/289/P